First Print Edition [1.0] -1438 h. (2017 c.e.)

Copyright © 1438 H./2017 C.E.
Taalib al-Ilm Educational Resources

http://taalib.com
Learn Islaam, Live Islaam.^{SM}

ISBN EAN-13:   978-1-93811-759-6   [Soft cover Print Edition]

Golden Words Upon Golden Words...For Every Muslim.

"Imaam al-Barbahaaree, may Allaah have mercy upon him said:

May Allaah have mercy upon you! Examine carefully the speech of everyone you hear from in your time particularly. So do not act in haste and do not enter into anything from it until you ask and see: Did any of the Companions of the Prophet, may Allaah's praise and salutations be upon him, speak about it, or did any of the scholars? So if you find a narration from them about it, cling to it, do not go beyond it for anything and do not give precedence to anything over it and thus fall into the Fire.

Explanation by Sheikh Saaleh al-Fauzaan, may Allaah preserve him:

'Do not be hasty in accepting as correct what you may hear from the people, especially in these later times. As now there are many who speak about so many various matters, issuing rulings and ascribing to themselves both knowledge and the right to speak. This is especially the case after the emergence and spread of new modern day media technologies. Such that everyone now can speak and bring forth that which is, in truth, worthless; by this, meaning words of no true value - speaking about whatever they wish in the name of knowledge and in the name of the religion of Islaam. It has even reached the point that you find the people of misguidance and the members of the various groups of misguidance and deviance from the religion speaking as well. Such individuals have now become those who speak in the name of the religion of Islaam through means such as the various satellite television channels. Therefore be very cautious!

It is upon you, oh Muslim, and upon you, oh student of knowledge, individually, to verify matters and not rush to embrace everything and anything you may hear. It is upon you to verify the truth of what you hear, asking, 'Who else also makes this same statement or claim?', 'Where did this thought or concept originate or come from?', 'Who is its reference or source authority?' Asking what are the evidences which support it from within the Book and the Sunnah? And inquiring where has the individual who is putting this forth studied and taken his knowledge from? From who has he studied the knowledge of Islaam?

Each of these matters requires verification through inquiry and investigation, especially in the present age and time. It is not every speaker who should rightly be considered a source of knowledge, even if he is well spoken and eloquent and can manipulate words captivating his listeners. Do not be taken in and accept him until you are aware of the degree and scope of what he possesses of knowledge and understanding. Perhaps someone's words may be few, but possess true understanding, and perhaps another will have a great deal of speech yet he is actually ignorant to such a degree that he doesn't actually possess anything of true understanding. Rather he only has the ability to enchant with his speech so that the people are deceived. Yet he puts forth the perception that he is a scholar, that he is someone of true understanding and comprehension, that he is a capable thinker, and so forth. Through such means and ways he is able to deceive and beguile the people, taking them away from the way of truth.

Therefore, what is to be given true consideration is not the amount of the speech put forth or that one can extensively discuss a subject. Rather, the criterion that is to be given consideration is what that speech contains within it of sound authentic knowledge, what it contains of the established and transmitted principles of Islaam. Perhaps a short or brief statement which is connected to or has a foundation in the established principles can be of greater benefit than a great deal of speech which simply rambles on, and through hearing you don't actually receive very much benefit from.

This is the reality which is present in our time; one sees a tremendous amount of speech which only possesses within it a small amount of actual knowledge. We see the presence of many speakers, yet few people of true understanding and comprehension.' "

[The eminent major scholar Sheikh Saaleh al-Fauzaan, may Allaah preserve him- 'A Valued Gift for the Reader Of Comments Upon the Book Sharh as-Sunnah', page 102-103]

❴ *Is not He better than your so-called gods, He Who originates creation and shall then repeat it, and Who provides for you from heaven and earth? Is there any god with Allaah? Say: 'Bring forth your proofs, if you are truthful.'* ❵-(Surah an-Naml: 64)

Explanation: ❴ *Say: "Bring forth your proofs.."* ❵ This is a command for the Prophet, may Allaah's praise and salutation be upon him, to rebuke them immediately after they had put forward their own rebuke. Meaning: '*Say to them: bring your proof, whether it is an intellectual proof or a proof from transmitted knowledge, that would stand as evidence that there is another with Allaah, the Most Glorified and the Most Exalted*. Additionally, it has been said that it means: '*Bring your proof that there is anyone other than Allaah, the Most High, who is capable of doing that which has been mentioned from His actions, the Most Glorified and the Most Exalted.*' ❴ *...if you are truthful.* ❵ meaning, in this claim. From this it is derived that a claim is not accepted unless clearly indicated by evidences."

[*Tafseer al-'Aloosee: vol. 15, page 14*]

Sheikh Rabee'a Ibn Hadee Umair al-Madkhalee, may Allaah preserve him said,

'It is possible for someone to simply say, "*So and so said such and such.*" However we should say, "*Produce your proof.*" So why did you not ask them for their proof by saying to them: "*Where was this said?*" Ask them questions such as this, as from your weapons are such questions as: "*Where is this from? From which book? From which cassette?...*" '

[*The Overwhelming Falsehoods of 'Abdul-Lateef Bashmeel' page 14*]

The guiding scholar Imaam Sheikh 'Abdul-'Azeez Ibn Abdullah Ibn Baaz, may Allaah have mercy upon him, said,

'It is not proper that any intelligent individual be misled or deceived by the great numbers from among people from the various countries who engage in such a practice. As the truth is not determined by the numerous people who engage in a matter, rather the truth is known by the Sharee'ah evidences. Just as Allaah the Most High says in Surah al-Baqarah, ❴ *And they say, "None shall enter Paradise unless he be a Jew or a Christian." These are only their own desires. Say "Produce your proof if you are truthful."* ❵-(Surah al-Baqarah: 111) And Allaah the Most High says ❴ *And if you obey most of those on the earth, they will mislead you far away from Allaah's path. They follow nothing but conjectures, and they do nothing but lie.* ❵-(Surah al-'Ana'an: 116)'

[*Collection of Rulings and Various Statements of Sheikh Ibn Baaz -Vol. 1 page 85*]

Sheikh Muhammad Ibn 'Abdul-Wahaab, may Allaah have mercy upon him, said,

'Additionally, verify that knowledge held regarding your beliefs, distinguishing between what is correct and false within it, coming to understand the various areas of knowledge of faith in Allaah alone and the required disbelief in all other objects of worship. You will certainly see various different matters which are called towards and enjoined; so if you see that a matter is in fact one coming from Allaah and His Messenger, then this is what is intended and is desired that you possess. Otherwise, Allaah has certainly given you that which enables you to distinguish between truth and falsehood, if Allaah so wills.

Moreover, this writing of mine- do not conceal it from the author of that work; rather present it to him. He may repent and affirm its truthfulness and then return to the guidance of Allaah, or perhaps if he says that he has a proof for his claims, even if that is only a single statement, or if he claims that within my statements there is something unsupported, then request his evidence for that assertion. After this if there is something which continues to cause uncertainty or is a problem for you, then refer it back to me, so that then you are aware of both his statement and mine in that issue. We ask Allaah to guide us, you, and all the Muslims to that which He loves and is pleased with.'

[Personal Letters of Sheikh Muhammad Ibn 'Abdul-Wahaab- Conclusion to Letter 20]

Sheikh 'Abdullah Ibn 'Abdur-Rahman Abu Bateen, may Allaah have mercy upon him, said,

'And for an individual, if it becomes clear to him that something is the truth, he should not turn away from it and or be discouraged simply due to the few people who agree with him and the many who oppose him in that, especially in these latter days of this present age.

If the ignorant one says: "*If this was the truth so and so and so and so would have been aware of it!*" However this is the very claim of the disbelievers, in their statement found in the Qur'aan ◈ *If it had truly been good, they would not have preceded us to it!* ◈-(Surah al-Ahqaaf: 11) and in their statement ◈ *Is it these whom Allaah has favored from amongst us?* ◈-(Surah al-Ana'am: 53). Yet certainly, as Alee Ibn Abee Taalib, may Allaah be pleased with him, stated "*Know the truth and then you will know it' people.*" But for the one who generally stands upon confusion and uncertainty, then every doubt swirls around him. And if the majority of the people were in fact upon the truth today, then Islaam would not be considered strange, yet, by Allaah, it is today seen as the most strange of affairs!"

[Durar As-Sanneeyyah -vol. 10, page 400]

30 Days of Guidance:
SignPosts Towards Rectification & Repentance

A Short Journey through Selected Questions & Answers
with Sheikh Muhammad Ibn Saaleh al-'Utheimeen

[Exercise Workbook]

Compiled and Translated by:
Abu Sukhailah Khalil Ibn-Abelahyi

[4] CHARACTER & MANNERS

```
Student name:_____

Date started:_____

Date completed:_____

Online login:_____

Online pass:_____
```

How to use this Exercise Workbook

This workbook can be used to make it simpler for the one administering a study circle to check all exercise homewor from the answer key which is available at the back of the [Self-Study / Teachers Edition].The exercise workbooks can be collected after class or at another convenient time for student work to be checked before proceeding to the next day.

A small marking area has been added for indicating correct and incorrect answers at the bottom of each page. Depending on question type , there is a [/ 1] or [/ 3] for recording the number of correct answers out of total answers on that specific page. Partial scores can be given for essay answers that may not completely fulfill the needed answer, and then clarifying notes added in the teacher notes section below the same essay answer area. In addition, there is also an final total correct area i.e. =[/ 15] at the end of each day's section for recording the total number of correct answers for each individual day's exercises.

SCORING EACH DAYS EXERCISE ASSESSMENT TOTAL

Multiply the total points of correct answers (max. 15) times (X) 6.7 for score out of 100.

Sheikh Muhammad Ibn Saaleh al-'Utheimeen, may Allaah have mercy upon him, said,

"….Firstly, I congratulate you on Allaah guiding you to repentance, and your success in turning to Allaah in repentance. I ask Allaah, the Most High, to make you steadfast on this, that He bless all of us to make that needed true sincere repentance by which Allaah wipes away what we previously committed of sins, and that He protect us in what comes in the future.

Secondly, I give you glad tiding, you should know that your repentance has erased what you previous committed of sins, and you do not need to further make up for happened in the past. But you should ask and beseech Allaah to bless you with steadfastness upon obeying Him until the time that you reach finally Him.

Moreover, you should endeavor as much as you are able to, to invite and call your previous companions who are still similar to how you used to be, to the same goodness of repentance that Allaah blessed you yourself with, and toward their also choosing to hold firmly to Allaah's straight path. As the Messenger of Allaah, may the praise and salutations of Allaah be upon him said, *{That through you a single individual is guided is better that your receiving a valuable red camel.}*

As from your own thankfulness towards Allaah for His guiding you, is that you strive to guide your previous companions or brothers, those who are still wasting their own lives, towards the true repentance, and struggling to be steadfast upon the religion of Allaah."

(From Fataawaa Nur 'Alaa ad-Darb lil Fadheelatul Sheikh al-Allaamah Muhammad Ibn Saaleh al-'Utheimeen: vol 12, pg. 90)

TABLE OF CONTENTS

THE "30 DAYS OF GUIDANCE" SERIES

The goal of the "*30 Days of Guidance*" book series is to better enable us, as worshipers of Allaah, to embody and reflect in the various different areas of life for a Muslim, our connection and adherence to the believer's path of the first three believing generations. Many Muslims, due to lacking opportunities to study consistently and be cultivated at the feet of noble steadfast scholars, have an inconsistency they themselves recognize- an inconsistency between the clear path of Islaam of the first Muslims, which they have connected themselves to, and what they have actually been successful in making a daily reality in their practice of Islaam. Sheikh Saaleh Ibn al-Fauzaan, may Allaah preserve him, explained the importance of striving to rectify this,

"... For the one who proceeds upon the methodology of the best generations, even if that is during the very last days of the existence of earth, then he is safe, saved, and protected from entering the Hellfire. As Allaah, the Most Glorified and the Most Exalted, said, ❨***And the first to embrace Islaam of the Muhaajiroon (those who migrated from Makkah to Al-Madinah) and the Ansaar (the citizens of Al-Madinah who helped and gave aid to the Muhaajiroon) and also those who followed them exactly (in faith). Allaah is well-pleased with them as they are well-pleased with Him. He has prepared for them Gardens under which rivers flow (Paradise), to dwell therein forever. That is the supreme success.***❩*–(Surah Al-Tawbah:100)*

*So Allaah, the Most Exalted, the Most Magnificent, has included and described them as those who follow Muhaajiroon and the Ansaar, upon a condition, "**who followed them exactly (in faith)**." Meaning truly followed them with precision and integrity, not merely putting forth a claim or outwardly attributing or attaching themselves to them without actually realizing their guidance. This is true whether that shortfall is caused by ignorance or by the following of desires. Not everyone who attributes himself to the first three generations is true in his assertion unless he follows them precisely and with integrity. This is in fact a condition, a condition placed by Allaah, the Most Glorified and the Most Exalted. The wording "**exactly (in faith).** meaning precisely, with integrity, as well as entirely.*

What is required in truly following them is that you study the methodology of the Salaf, that you understand it, and that you are firmly attached to it. But as for individuals who simply attribute themselves to them, while they do not really understand their methodology nor their way, then this does not really benefit them with anything, and does not actually help them in any way. Such people are not from those upon the way of the Salaf and should not be considered Salafees, because they are not following the first generations precisely with integrity, as indeed Allaah, the Most Glorified and the Most Exalted, has placed this as the condition for their following of them to be true.

....The one who proceeds upon the methodology of the Salaf must have two characteristics, as we have previously mentioned. Firstly, actually understanding the methodology of the first generations, and the second matter is adhering firmly to it, even when it causes him hardship and discomfort. As he will certainly encounter a great deal of that from those who oppose this path of guidance. He will encounter harassment. He will encounter stubbornness. He will encounter false accusations. He will face having directed towards him evil names and false labels. However, he must remain patient in the face of this, as he is convinced and satisfied with what he stands upon. He should be not shaken or troubled in the face of a whirlwind of difficulties. He should not be affected or changed by what he encounters of different trials, but remains patient when facing them until he meets his Lord.

Accordingly, one must firstly learn the methodology of the first three generations, and then follow it exactly with integrity, while being patient with what he encounters from the people due to this adherence. Yet this, in and of itself, is also not enough; it is additionally necessary to spread the methodology of the first generations. It is required to invite the people to Allaah and invite them to the way of the Salaf, to explain it to the people and spread this way among them. The one who does this is Salafee in reality and truth. But as for the one who claims Salafeeyah, yet he does not truly understand the methodology of the Salaf, or he does indeed understand it yet fails to truly follow it, but simply follows what the people are upon, or merely follows what happens to agree with his desires, this one is not Salafee, even if he calls and labels himself that.

This fact demands from us that we place great importance in fully comprehending the way of the first generations and studying their methodology in beliefs, character, and actions in every environment and situation. As the path and methodology of the first three generations is that methodology upon which the Messenger of Allaah, may the praise and salutations be upon him, was upon, and is that way which those who follow the best of generations and walk upon their path, will proceed upon until the Final Hour is established....

...As such, it is required that the one who claims this way, or connects himself to the Salaf make this descriptive name a reality and make his attachment to them something which truly reflects the way of the first generations in beliefs, and in statements, and in actions, and in general dealings so that he may be a true Salafee and that he may be a righteous example to others and someone who sincerely reflects the way of the righteous first generations of Islaam." [1]

We ask Allaah for success in each of our efforts to both learn and reflect the clear path of the first three generations, in every area of our individual lives, the lives of our spouses, and the lives of our children. And the success is from Allaah.

---

[1]   From the lecture "Salafeeyah, Its Reality And Its Characteristics" http://www.alfawzan.af.org.sa/

DAY 1: HOW DO I WORK TO SAVE MYSELF FROM HELLFIRE?

TEST YOUR UNDERSTANDING

3 min

TRUE & FALSE QUESTIONS

[Circle the correct letter for each individual sentence from today's content.]

01. A Muslim should hope that Allaah will save him from Hellfire, [T / F] and enter him into Paradise, just because Allaah is merciful.

02. Once someone is guided there is no danger of them becoming [T / F] misguided in the future.

03. Each Muslim who truly strives to be righteous is generally [T / F] given good in both this life and in the Hereafter.

6 min

FILL IN THE BLANK QUESTIONS

[Enter the correct individual words to complete the sentences from today's content.]

04. A believer _____ to be blessed with Allaah's _____, and be _____ from Hellfire.

05. A Muslim's _____ is based upon what he puts forth of the _____ of Allaah alone without associating any _____ with Him.

06. We worship Allaah by _____ out whatever Allaah has _____, and _____ away from everything that Allaah has _____.

1.

COMPREHENSIVE UNDERSTANDING QUESTIONS

7-12 min

07. Give an example of a blameworthy matter or condition within one's heart that might prevent Allaah from accepting his deeds.

_____

_____

_____

_____

_____

_____

_____

_____

_____

_____

_____

_____

_____

_____

_____

_____

_____

_____

_____

_____

_____

_____

_____

TEACHER NOTES / CORRECTIONS

_____

_____

_____

_____

*[/ 3]

7-12min

08. Give an example of two blameworthy matters or conditions within one's outward actions that might prevent Allaah from accepting his deeds.

_____

_____

_____

_____

_____

_____

_____

_____

_____

_____

_____

_____

_____

_____

_____

_____

_____

_____

_____

_____

_____

_____

_____

_____

_____

TEACHER NOTES / CORRECTIONS

_____

_____

_____

_____

7-12min

09. List three examples of actions done by the people who have of taqwa, whom Allaah rewards, mentioned in the lesson.

_____

_____

_____

_____

_____

_____

_____

_____

_____

_____

_____

_____

_____

_____

_____

_____

_____

_____

_____

_____

_____

_____

_____

_____

TEACHER NOTES / CORRECTIONS

_____

_____

_____

_____

_____

_____

✱[/ 3]=[/ 15]

DAY 2: WHAT SHOULD I DO, AS MY SOCIETY HAS A GREAT DEAL WRONGDOING AND SINNING?

TEST YOUR UNDERSTANDING

TRUE & FALSE QUESTIONS

[Circle the correct letter for each individual sentence from today's content.]

3 min

01. A Muslim should not worry about being affected by the different people around him in society. [T / F]

02. What is most important for a Muslim to focus upon is being successful within society, both economically and politically. [T / F]

03. Every individual being satisfied and pleased generally with his own opinions and personal views is a sign of misguidance in a society. [T / F]

FILL IN THE BLANK QUESTIONS

[Enter the correct individual words to complete the sentences from today's content.]

6 min

04. A Muslim should _____ to live within his society according to the guidance of _____, and invite to the _____ of Allaah, with _____ and good admonition.

05. He should _____ upon _____ and saving himself, and leaving alone the situation of the _____ people, when he sees _____ generally followed.

06. The _____ believer understands the best way to live his life as a _____, and how to _____ himself from the _____ of those different types of people whose are misguided.

COMPREHENSIVE UNDERSTANDING QUESTIONS

07.   Give two specific examples of people giving more importance to material or financial concerns than righteous deeds and the worship of Allaah.

TEACHER NOTES / CORRECTIONS

08. Give two specific examples of how a Muslim might work to safeguard himself and his family within a corrupt society.

TEACHER NOTES / CORRECTIONS

09. Give two specific examples of possible ways a Muslim might protect himself from the harm of the misguided people they need to interact with regularly.

TEACHER NOTES / CORRECTIONS

*[/3]=[/15]

DAY 3: HOW CAN I UNDERSTAND WHAT TAQWA IS, AND HAVE IT IN MY LIFE?

DAY - 03

TEST YOUR UNDERSTANDING

TRUE & FALSE QUESTIONS

[Circle the correct letter for each individual sentence from today's content.]

3 min

01. The person with the most taqwa was the Messenger of Allaah. [T / F]

02. It is not actually part of taqwa is that a person turns away from [T / F] whatever Allaah has made impermissible.

03. Taqwa is that an individual undertakes that which will protect [T / F] them from the punishment of Allaah.

FILL IN THE BLANK QUESTIONS

[Enter the correct individual words to complete the sentences from today's content.]

6 min

04. A Muslim acting with _____ requires _____ and understanding.

05. Part of taqwa is that a person _____ whatever has been _____ by Allaah.

06. Part of _____ is that a person _____ _____ from whatever Allaah has made _____. .

COMPREHENSIVE UNDERSTANDING QUESTIONS

7-12min

07. Give three specific examples of actions which are from taqwa in relation to obligations for a Muslim.

_____

_____

_____

_____

_____

_____

_____

_____

_____

_____

_____

_____

_____

_____

_____

_____

_____

_____

_____

_____

_____

_____

_____

TEACHER NOTES / CORRECTIONS

_____

_____

_____

_____

_____

*[/3]

08. Give three specific examples of actions which are from taqwa in relation a Muslim avoiding prohibited matters.

TEACHER NOTES / CORRECTIONS

09. Give one example of something specific a Muslim could do to help increase their personal taqwa.

TEACHER NOTES / CORRECTIONS

✳[/3]=[/15]

TEST YOUR UNDERSTANDING

TRUE & FALSE QUESTIONS

[Circle the correct letter for each individual sentence from today's content.]

3min

01. When a Muslim calls himself to account, he questions himself   [T / F]
    about his statements and deeds.

02. A Muslim only needs to consider why he didn't fulfil those   [T / F]
    obligations he should have.

03. Fulfilling those matters which Allaah has made obligatory upon   [T / F]
    us does not strengthen our faith.

FILL IN THE BLANK QUESTIONS

[Enter the correct individual words to complete the sentences from today's content.]

6min

04. An example of self-questioning is asking, "*Why didn't I do what I knew was*
    _____ *and* _____ *at this time or in this situation?*"

05. An example of self-questioning is asking, "*What I said at this time and*
    _____ *was certainly* _____ *and* _____."

06. _____ about the _____ of the Prophet and his
    noble Companions _____ our hearts, minds and intellects as
    Muslims.

COMPREHENSIVE UNDERSTANDING QUESTIONS

7-12 min

DAY - 04

07.   Give examples of three obligations that a Muslim might take himself to account for neglecting in our age.

TEACHER NOTES / CORRECTIONS

✳[/ 3]

08. Give examples of three prohibited matters that a Muslim might take himself to account for doing in our age.

TEACHER NOTES / CORRECTIONS

09. For three mentioned general beneficial acts, that a Muslim engages in order to gain closeness to Allaah, give specific examples of when they might be done within a busy schedule.

TEACHER NOTES / CORRECTIONS

✳[/ 3]=[/ 15]

TEST YOUR UNDERSTANDING

TRUE & FALSE QUESTIONS

[Circle the correct letter for each individual sentence from today's content.]

01. A Muslim should only intend the reward of Jannah in whatever [T / F] he does of good deeds.

02. The mentioned verse only discusses a single goal or aim the [T / F] Muslim has in making ritual prayer.

03. There is no contradiction in intending several good objectives [T / F] of a good deed, at the same time.

FILL IN THE BLANK QUESTIONS

[Enter the correct individual words to complete the sentences from today's content.]

04. It is _____ to have sincerity for Allaah _____, when _____ to do an act of _____.

05. In doing a good deed, a Muslim might seek to _____ an _____ upon him.

06. In doing a good deed, a Muslim might seek the _____ of _____ in the Hereafter.

COMPREHENSIVE UNDERSTANDING QUESTIONS

7-12 min

DAY - 05

07.   Give a specific example, of a good deed that a Muslim may undertake in their interactions with their spouse, and two possible good intentions they might have in doing that.

_____

_____

_____

_____

_____

_____

_____

_____

_____

_____

_____

_____

_____

_____

_____

_____

_____

_____

_____

_____

_____

_____

_____

_____

_____

TEACHER NOTES / CORRECTIONS

_____

_____

_____

_____

✳[/3]

08.   Give a specific example, of a good deed that a Muslim may undertake in their interactions with their spouse, and two possible good intents they might have in doing that.

_____

_____

_____

_____

_____

_____

_____

_____

_____

_____

_____

_____

_____

_____

_____

_____

_____

_____

_____

_____

_____

_____

TEACHER NOTES / CORRECTIONS

_____

_____

_____

_____

_____

09. Give a specific example, of a good deed that a Muslim may undertake in his dealing within his Muslim community, and two possible good intentions he might have in doing that.

TEACHER NOTES / CORRECTIONS

✳[/3]=[/15]

TEST YOUR UNDERSTANDING

3min

TRUE & FALSE QUESTIONS

[Circle the correct letter for each individual sentence from today's content.]

01. It is enough to strive to obey Allaah's commands in all things, [T / F] then Shaytaan cannot affect or harm you.

02. Striving to have a pure intention in the good deeds we do is [T / F] something easy.

03. We cannot do anything to protect ourselves from the whispers [T / F] of Shaytaan.

6min

FILL IN THE BLANK QUESTIONS

[Enter the correct individual words to complete the sentences from today's content.]

04. A person can be _____ and _____ by the _____ that Shaytaan directs at their heart.

05. We gain protection by seeking _____ in _____ from _____ the one who is accursed.

06. If someone is truly _____ if their efforts to do good, then Allaah, the Most High will make him _____.

COMPREHENSIVE UNDERSTANDING QUESTIONS

7-12 min

07.   Give two examples of two good outward actions that may require more effort in purifying your sincere intention for Allaah alone.

DAY - 06

_____

_____

_____

_____

_____

_____

_____

_____

_____

_____

_____

_____

_____

_____

_____

_____

_____

_____

_____

_____

_____

_____

_____

_____

_____

_____

TEACHER NOTES / CORRECTIONS

_____

_____

_____

_____

∗[/ 3]

7-12 min

08. Give an example of a good deed that might be done in a specific way that may better protects your pure intention from being attacked by the whispers of Shaytaan.

_____

_____

_____

_____

_____

_____

_____

_____

_____

_____

_____

_____

_____

_____

_____

_____

_____

_____

_____

_____

_____

_____

_____

TEACHER NOTES / CORRECTIONS

_____

_____

_____

_____

_____

09. Give an example of a good deed that Shaytaan might work to turn you away from with his deceptive and false whispers, where having patience upon achieving it produces beneficial results.

7-12 min

TEACHER NOTES / CORRECTIONS

*[/ 3]=[/ 15]

TEST YOUR UNDERSTANDING

TRUE & FALSE QUESTIONS

[Circle the correct letter for each individual sentence from today's content.]

3 min

01. Focusing only on the worldly life makes bringing ease to your   [T / F]
     heart when troubled more difficult.

02. A person who puts forth considerable effort to bring good to   [T / F]
     himself generally has a heart more at ease.

03. Loving someone for the sake of Allaah is connected to what we   [T / F]
     see from them individually of striving for Allaah

FILL IN THE BLANK QUESTIONS

[Enter the correct individual words to complete the sentences from today's content.]

6 min

04. Engaging   in   the   _____   of   Allaah,   helps   remove   the
     _____ and pain we feel in our _____,

05. There are _____ general reasons for having _____
     for someone not connected to _____.

06. The _____ type of love, which is for Allaah's sake, is from the
     _____ and _____ forms of love.

COMPREHENSIVE UNDERSTANDING QUESTIONS

7-12 min

07.   Give an example of a specific situation, which may happen to someone personally, where engaging in the remembrance of Allaah may bring their heart ease.

DAY - 07

_____
_____
_____
_____
_____
_____
_____
_____
_____
_____
_____
_____
_____
_____
_____
_____
_____
_____
_____
_____
_____
_____

TEACHER NOTES / CORRECTIONS

_____
_____
_____
_____
_____

*[/3]

7-12 min

08. Give the example of three outward acts that you may see a Muslim doing which cause you to love them more for Allaah's sake.

_____
_____
_____
_____
_____
_____
_____
_____
_____
_____
_____
_____
_____
_____
_____
_____
_____
_____
_____
_____
_____
_____
_____

TEACHER NOTES / CORRECTIONS

_____
_____
_____
_____
_____

[/ 3]✻

09.   Give an example of someone righteous who you might love only for the sake of Allaah in this life, in order to gain closeness to them in the next life.

7-12 min

_____

TEACHER NOTES / CORRECTIONS

*[/ 3]=[/ 15]

TEST YOUR UNDERSTANDING

TRUE & FALSE QUESTIONS

[Circle the correct letter for each individual sentence from today's content.]

01. It is not possible for someone to always remain at a constant [T / F] level in their emaan or faith.

02. The Messenger of Allaah taught the Companions that every [T / F] matter has its own proper time.

03. The only focus a Muslim should have is making sure he is [T / F] doing good deeds according to the Sunnah.

FILL IN THE BLANK QUESTIONS

[Enter the correct individual words to complete the sentences from today's content.]

04. Every person will encounter times of _____ in performing the _____ of Allaah.

05. Every Muslim must strive to _____ his heart from _____, and from anything related to _____ others with Allaah in _____.

06. We have been commanded with different acts of _____ at different _____ of the day in order to _____ our _____ of Allaah.

COMPREHENSIVE UNDERSTANDING QUESTIONS

7-12 min

07. Give examples of three specific acts of personal worship someone might perform during the day that are found in the Sunnah.

TEACHER NOTES / CORRECTIONS

*[/3]

08. Give examples of three permissible activities within his day that a Muslim might do or undertake with his family.

TEACHER NOTES / CORRECTIONS

09. Give a specific example of something within a Muslim's heart which if not struggled against, will cause some harm to their practice of Islaam. Explain how their practice of Islaam is better due to working to remove it.

TEACHER NOTES / CORRECTIONS

*[/3]=[/15]

TEST YOUR UNDERSTANDING

TRUE & FALSE QUESTIONS

[Circle the correct letter for each individual sentence from today's content.]

DAY - 09

3min

01. Once we are guided to be upon Islaam, then alhamdulillah [T / F] there in no more need to be concerned.

02. A Muslim only needs to fulfill the outward aspects of the five [T / F] pillars of Islaam to remain successful.

03. When we feel our emaan, or faith, is weak, the only remedy is [T / F] to supplicate to Allaah for help.

FILL IN THE BLANK QUESTIONS

[Enter the correct individual words to complete the sentences from today's content.]

6min

04. Every person can _____ according to what their hearts _____, what their eyes _____, and what their ears _____.

05. It is important as a Muslim to ask Allaah, the Most High, _____ for _____ in your religion.

06. A Muslim should not focus upon the _____ of what they used to be upon of _____ and sinning , but look to what is in front of them of _____ for _____, obedience, and a tremendous _____.

COMPREHENSIVE UNDERSTANDING QUESTIONS

7-12 min

07.   Give two possible practical examples of the benefit a Muslim gains by having associates and friends who are committed to being steadfast in Islaam.

DAY - 09

TEACHER NOTES / CORRECTIONS

✳[/ 3]

7-12min

08. Give two possible practical harmful situations a Muslim faces by having associates and friends who are either non-muslims or Muslims who are very lax in their practice of Islaam.

TEACHER NOTES / CORRECTIONS

09. Give two personal examples related to your life of beneficial endeavors or permissible goals you want to accomplish as a Muslim in the future, inshAllaah.

TEACHER NOTES / CORRECTIONS

*[/ 3]=[/ 15]

TEST YOUR UNDERSTANDING

DAY - 10

TRUE & FALSE QUESTIONS

[Circle the correct letter for each individual sentence from today's content.]

01. One thing that helps a Muslim soften a hardened heart is [T / F] reading and reciting the Qur'aan.

02. One benefit to learning about the life history of the Prophet [T / F] Muhammad is how it affects us inwardly, and reminds us.

03. Beneficial poetry is something which may be good for the heart [T / F] of a Muslim.

FILL IN THE BLANK QUESTIONS

[Enter the correct individual words to complete the sentences from today's content.]

04. Someone with a hardened heart may find that they _____ humility and _____ in their obligatory ritual _____.

05. From the causes of the softening of the heart, is maintaining one's _____ and _____ of heart during the ritual _____.

06. Treating _____ with _____ and interacting with them with _____ can soften the hardened heart.

COMPREHENSIVE UNDERSTANDING QUESTIONS

7-12 min

07. What are two practical examples of ways or times that we can listen to beneficial reminders which help our hearts remain healthy?

TEACHER NOTES / CORRECTIONS

*[/3]

08. Give a specific example of someone whose perspective and actions in their daily life leads to their heart not being healthy.

TEACHER NOTES / CORRECTIONS

09. Give a specific example of the general meaning of an authentic hadeeth or narration about life history of the Prophet or his Companions that you personally benefited from as a Muslim.

_____
_____
_____
_____
_____
_____
_____
_____
_____
_____
_____
_____
_____
_____
_____
_____
_____
_____
_____
_____
_____
_____
_____
_____

TEACHER NOTES / CORRECTIONS

_____
_____
_____
_____
_____

✳[/ 3]=[/ 15]

TEST YOUR UNDERSTANDING

TRUE & FALSE QUESTIONS

[Circle the correct letter for each individual sentence from today's content.]

3min

DAY - 11

01. It is important to review what you have memorized from the Qur'aan. [T / F]

02. Neglecting to review and maintain your memorization of the Qur'aan is a sin for a Muslim. [T / F]

03. As long as we are not doing what is forbidden, how we use our time isn't really important. [T / F]

FILL IN THE BLANK QUESTIONS

[Enter the correct individual words to complete the sentences from today's content.]

6min

04. The Muslim who _____ himself to reciting the Qur'aan regularly receives a _____ from that and keeps a strong _____ to the Word of Allaah.

05. The one who neglects the _____, actually forgetting what they had _____, has fallen into a _____ sin.

06. The Prophet of Allaah, may the praise and salutations of Allaah be upon him, warned us that our _____ of the Qur'aan could easily slip away if not _____.

COMPREHENSIVE UNDERSTANDING QUESTIONS

7-12 min

07.   Give two possible ways that we can encourage our families to be consistent in their memorization and reading of the Qur'aan.

DAY - 11

TEACHER NOTES / CORRECTIONS

✱[/3]

08. Give a general example of something often studied today that people give precedence to over focusing on the Qur'aan.

_____

_____

_____

_____

_____

_____

_____

_____

_____

_____

_____

_____

_____

_____

_____

_____

_____

_____

_____

_____

_____

_____

_____

DAY - 11

TEACHER NOTES / CORRECTIONS

_____

_____

_____

_____

_____

_____

09. Give a specific example of one possible benefit that comes from maintaining a strong connection to the Qur'aan.

TEACHER NOTES / CORRECTIONS

✱[/ 3]=[/ 15]

TEST YOUR UNDERSTANDING

TRUE & FALSE QUESTIONS

[Circle the correct letter for each individual sentence from today's content.]

3 min

01. It is an obligation to listen and pay attention to the Friday [T / F] khutbah when you attend Jumu'ah.

02. Some of the distractions that we encounter are directed at us [T / F] for a specific goal.

03. There are specific things we should do in order to benefit from [T / F] the khutbah on Jumu'ah.

FILL IN THE BLANK QUESTIONS

[Enter the correct individual words to complete the sentences from today's content.]

6 min

04. The Muslim who attends Jumu'ah prayer in the _____, should _____ to the _____ of the imaam.

05. During _____, Muslims should work to stop inward _____, and _____ upon their worship comfortably, not being distracted or _____.

06. Allaah has warned us against being like those whose hearts He has _____, those who _____ their lusts or evil _____.

COMPREHENSIVE UNDERSTANDING QUESTIONS

7-12min

07.   Give an example of one practical way to avoid being distracted by things during Jumu'ah.

DAY - 12

TEACHER NOTES / CORRECTIONS

08. Give an unmentioned possible example of how Shaytaan might distract you from something which contains benefit and good for you in your life as a Muslim. How could you prevent or lessen that distraction?

DAY - 12

TEACHER NOTES / CORRECTIONS

09. What effect might been seen in the lives of those Muslims who do not attend Jumu'ah at all when they are able to or come to Jumu'ah but generally pay little attention to the khutbah or the ritual prayer?

TEACHER NOTES / CORRECTIONS

*[/ 3]=[/ 15]

TEST YOUR UNDERSTANDING

TRUE & FALSE QUESTIONS

[Circle the correct letter for each individual sentence from today's content.]

3 min

01. Every Muslim will face challenges and problems in their striving   [T / F]
to live their life properly.

02. For true success, striving in doing outward good deeds should   [T / F]
be joined with inward good deeds and efforts.

03. It is better for a Muslim to just focus on the Arabic recitation   [T / F]
of the Qur'aan, whether he understands its meanings or not.

FILL IN THE BLANK QUESTIONS

[Enter the correct individual words to complete the sentences from today's content.]

6 min

04. A Muslim should choose companions, who have sound _____,
and who will _____ and strengthen him in his efforts to
practice _____.

05. Allaah can give new _____ to your practice of Islaam through
relying upon Him and having a strong _____ turn your
_____ towards Him alone.

06. The Muslim who proceeds with _____ and _____
will eventually be granted _____ and mastery in his efforts to
_____ Islaam.

COMPREHENSIVE UNDERSTANDING QUESTIONS

7-12 min

07. Give another example of something that a Muslim might encounter that clearly harms his efforts to properly practice Islaam. How could that possibly have been avoided?

DAY - 13

TEACHER NOTES / CORRECTIONS

✳[/3]

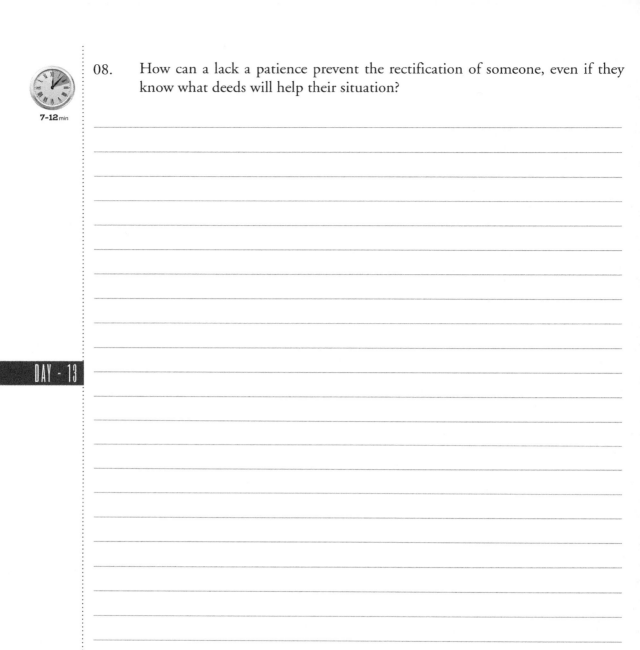

08. How can a lack a patience prevent the rectification of someone, even if they know what deeds will help their situation?

DAY - 13

TEACHER NOTES / CORRECTIONS

09. Give the example of another possible matter known from Islaam that may assist a person in rectifying weakness in his practice of Islaam.

TEACHER NOTES / CORRECTIONS

✳[/ 3]=[/ 15]

TEST YOUR UNDERSTANDING

TRUE & FALSE QUESTIONS

[Circle the correct letter for each individual sentence from today's content.]

3min

01. There are several different types of harm that may reach you [T / F] through reading fiction written by disbelievers.

02. As Muslims, we shouldn't take any knowledge at all from those [T / F] who reject Islaam.

03. Those Muslims who take beneficial knowledge from disbelievers, [T / F] must not allow this to negatively affect them inwardly.

FILL IN THE BLANK QUESTIONS

[Enter the correct individual words to complete the sentences from today's content.]

6min

04. Within the fictional stories produced by _____, there is a type of slow _____, and different types of _____ and corruption.

05. The various historical accounts coming from the _____ generations foster honor, nobility, _____ upon correct _____, and true _____ faith.

06. The popularity of western _____ among Muslims, gives them a _____ superiority and distinction of _____ over us.

[/6]✱   *064*

COMPREHENSIVE UNDERSTANDING QUESTIONS

7-12 min

07.   Give examples of three neutral areas of knowledge the Muslim Ummah can benefit from the non-Muslims within.

DAY - 14

TEACHER NOTES / CORRECTIONS

✴[/ 3]

08. What is one negative description of those Muslims who take disbelievers as friends and protectors, that Allaah mentions in the quoted verses?

TEACHER NOTES / CORRECTIONS

09.   How may learning more about the personalities and lives of the Muslims of the
        first three generations, help develop the faith of the Muslim inwardly?

TEACHER NOTES / CORRECTIONS

*[/3]=[/15]

TEST YOUR UNDERSTANDING

TRUE & FALSE QUESTIONS

[Circle the correct letter for each individual sentence from today's content.]

3 min

01. Some of the poetry people write, but not all poetry is accepted [T / F] in the guidance of Islaam.

02. Writing poetry is of the same value, or will bring us the same [T / F] reward as seeking knowledge.

03. A Muslim can write any kind of poetry they want, as it is just [T / F] words and personal expressions.

FILL IN THE BLANK QUESTIONS

[Enter the correct individual words to complete the sentences from today's content.]

04. Some poetry contains _____ for the Muslims, and _____ guide them to what is beneficial in their _____ and _____ affairs.

05. There is tremendous benefit in studying the _____ of Allaah, the _____ of the Messenger of Allaah, the statements of the _____, and the statements of the leading _____ who came after them.

06. One form of _____ poetry is that which legitimizes _____ and _____.

DAY - 15

6 min

COMPREHENSIVE UNDERSTANDING QUESTIONS

7-12 min

07. Give examples of two general activities a Muslim may focus on that may be permissible, but which are taking the place of something more beneficial for them.

DAY - 15

TEACHER NOTES / CORRECTIONS

✳[/3]

08. What is one possible explanation or excuse someone might give for their involvement in writing material that contain some aspect that is against the standards of Islaam?

TEACHER NOTES / CORRECTIONS

09. Give two specific example of possible subjects of poetry that someone might compose poetry about that would bring them a reward from Allaah.

TEACHER NOTES / CORRECTIONS

*[/3]=[/15]

TEST YOUR UNDERSTANDING

TRUE & FALSE QUESTIONS

[Circle the correct letter for each individual sentence from today's content.]

3 min

01. It is enough to just ignore or not pay attention to those bad   [T / F] thoughts which Shaytaan directs toward you.

02. There is a true blessing in a Muslim bringing to mind and   [T / F] remembering that Allaah guided them to strive to live properly upon Islaam.

03. There is never any harm in recalling the times or days before   [T / F] you were practicing Islaam properly

DAY - 16

FILL IN THE BLANK QUESTIONS

[Enter the correct individual words to complete the sentences from today's content.]

6 min

04. Whenever Shaytaan _____ to you, _____ seek _____ in Allaah from him.

05. Sometimes _____ about your days _____ striving upon Islaam might lead you back towards _____.

06. The Messenger of Allaah, may the praise and salutations of Allaah be upon him, before bringing them _____, found the Ansaar in a state of _____, poverty, and _____.

COMPREHENSIVE UNDERSTANDING QUESTIONS

7-12 min

07.   Give two practical examples of how Islaam can directly improve someone's life after they commit to it.

DAY - 16

TEACHER NOTES / CORRECTIONS

✳[/ 3]

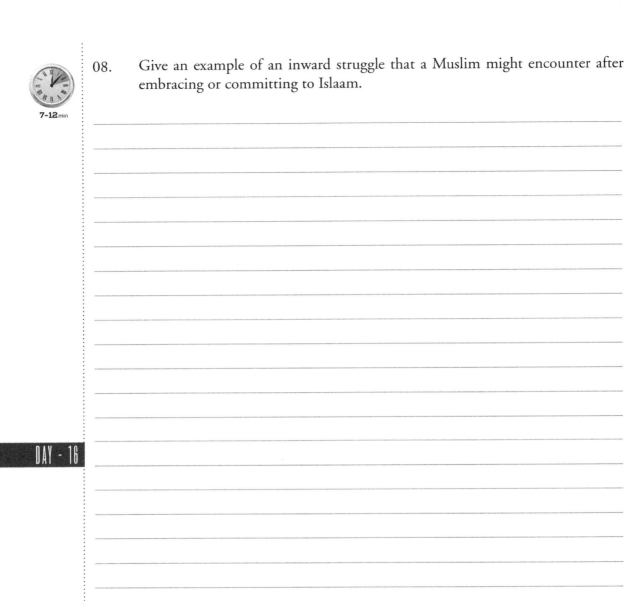

08. Give an example of an inward struggle that a Muslim might encounter after embracing or committing to Islaam.

DAY - 16

TEACHER NOTES / CORRECTIONS

09. How might previous friends, from before embracing Islaam, draw you back to old activities and priorities? What is a possible way that a Muslim could avoid and fight against this?

TEACHER NOTES / CORRECTIONS

*[/ 3]=[/ 15]

TEST YOUR UNDERSTANDING

TRUE & FALSE QUESTIONS

[Circle the correct letter for each individual sentence from today's content.]

3min

01. The company of a righteous Muslim helps us leave, and then   [T / F] remain away, from sins and transgressions.

02. As long as you have stopped a sin, such as smoking, there's no   [T / F] problem sitting with those who still do it.

03. It is important to inwardly call yourself to account and be   [T / F] determined, in order to leave a habit or practice which is forbidden, such as smoking.

DAY - 17

6min

FILL IN THE BLANK QUESTIONS

[Enter the correct individual words to complete the sentences from today's content.]

04. A Muslim who smokes can stop smoking _____, stage by _____, so that he reduces the _____ he smokes.

05. Once a Muslim _____ that smoking is _____, he should make a _____ to give up smoking.

06. When striving to be _____ upon Islaam, there is significant benefit in keeping _____ company with a _____ Muslim friend or associate.

COMPREHENSIVE UNDERSTANDING QUESTIONS

7-12 min

07.   List two different inward actions of a Muslim striving to leave a sinful practice, which the Sheikh discussed or mentioned within his answer.

DAY - 17

TEACHER NOTES / CORRECTIONS

*[/3]

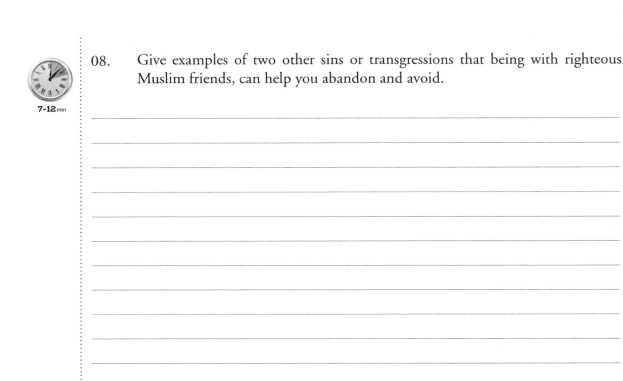

7-12 min

08.   Give examples of two other sins or transgressions that being with righteous Muslim friends, can help you abandon and avoid.

_____

_____

_____

_____

_____

_____

_____

_____

_____

_____

_____

_____

_____

_____

DAY - 17

_____

_____

_____

_____

_____

_____

_____

TEACHER NOTES / CORRECTIONS

_____

_____

_____

_____

_____

09. Give the example of a harmful environment or place that makes it difficult for a Muslim to remain steadfast in his practice of Islaam.

TEACHER NOTES / CORRECTIONS

*[/ 3]=[/ 15]

TEST YOUR UNDERSTANDING

TRUE & FALSE QUESTIONS

[Circle the correct letter for each individual sentence from today's content.]

3min

01.   If a Muslim neglected some obligatory prayers in the past, they   [T / F]
      need to make those up right away.

02.   The evil suggestions from Shaytaan cannot really affect us   [T / F]
      badly, as Allaah is merciful.

03.   We can say that there is only one act or type of adultery or   [T / F]
      fornication, which Islaam forbids.

FILL IN THE BLANK QUESTIONS

[Enter the correct individual words to complete the sentences from today's content.]

DAY - 18

6min

04.   When   a   young   Muslim   _____   generally   sees   young
      _____, he should _____ his eyesight and turn away.

05.   When Shaytaan _____ to us we should not _____
      it or _____ to it, nor let it affect our _____ to do
      what is good.

06.   It is _____ for a young Muslim to _____ praying
      the ritual prayer once they reach _____.

COMPREHENSIVE UNDERSTANDING QUESTIONS

7-12min

07. Give a specific example of another way that young people can fall into the sin of impermissibly looking at other young people. How could that have been avoided?

_____

_____

_____

_____

_____

_____

_____

_____

_____

_____

_____

_____

_____

_____

_____

_____

_____

_____

DAY - 18

_____

_____

_____

_____

_____

_____

_____

TEACHER NOTES / CORRECTIONS

_____

_____

_____

_____

_____

✳[/3]

08. What is a misconception about interacting with people of the opposite gender which is common today among some Muslims.

_____

_____

_____

_____

_____

_____

_____

_____

_____

_____

_____

_____

_____

_____

_____

_____

_____

_____

DAY - 18

_____

_____

_____

_____

_____

_____

_____

TEACHER NOTES / CORRECTIONS

_____

_____

_____

_____

_____

_____

09. How could adhering the prohibition of looking at unrelated women in public, prevent a Muslim from falling into a greater sin?

TEACHER NOTES / CORRECTIONS

*[/3]=[/15]

TEST YOUR UNDERSTANDING

TRUE & FALSE QUESTIONS

[Circle the correct letter for each individual sentence from today's content.]

3 min

01. If you think of some bad act but refrain and choose not to do it, you have still transgressed and sinned. [T / F]

02. The person's ritual worship is sound, even when distracting thoughts come, such that they need to struggle to focus upon their worship. [T / F]

03. The best option for a Muslim who is infatuated with someone permissible to marry, is to see if marriage to that person is possible for them. [T / F]

6 min

DAY - 19

FILL IN THE BLANK QUESTIONS

[Enter the correct individual words to complete the sentences from today's content.]

04. When A Muslim faces _____ thoughts about someone, they must _____ and struggle to _____ their _____ away from these thoughts.

05. If a Muslim finds themselves preoccupied with someone, they must _____ themselves from falling into what Allaah has made _____ towards that person or falling into improperly _____ with them.

06. Infatuation with someone may _____ you from properly engaging fully in the _____ of Allaah as well as pursuing those _____ endeavors that will _____ you.

COMPREHENSIVE UNDERSTANDING QUESTIONS

7-12min

07.   Give the example of one modern way that a Muslim could wrongly become infatuated with someone else without that other person even knowing it.

TEACHER NOTES / CORRECTIONS

✳[/ 3]

7-12 min

08. Give a general example of another possible negative effect of infatuation towards someone, if you are not within the process of contracting a permissible marriage with them.

_____

_____

_____

_____

_____

_____

_____

_____

_____

_____

_____

_____

_____

_____

_____

_____

_____

DAY - 19

_____

_____

_____

_____

_____

_____

TEACHER NOTES / CORRECTIONS

_____

_____

_____

_____

_____

_____

09.   Give an example of another situation where a Muslims might remind himself
       that. "Nothing good will come from this, so I need to stop it."

7-12 min

DAY - 19

TEACHER NOTES / CORRECTIONS

*[/3]=[/15]

TEST YOUR UNDERSTANDING

TRUE & FALSE QUESTIONS

[Circle the correct letter for each individual sentence from today's content.]

3 min

01. A sin or transgression in Islaam can be through doing something [T / F] or by abandoning or not doing something.

02. A Muslim should look towards the good coming from every [T / F] situation, even in their repentance from a sin.

03. It is not possible for a Muslim to gain strength of emaan, from [T / F] repenting and leaving wrongdoing, as they already committed a sin.

FILL IN THE BLANK QUESTIONS

[Enter the correct individual words to complete the sentences from today's content.]

6 min

DAY - 20

04. Every Muslim involved in some _____ or transgression should _____ turn towards making repentance _____ the _____ passes when they can do so.

05. Being _____ for a sin you committed, is one indication that your _____ from that was _____.

06. It is a _____ of repentance: that the individual have a firm _____ not to do, or commit, that transgression in the _____.

COMPREHENSIVE UNDERSTANDING QUESTIONS

7-12min

07.   Give two examples of transgressions that people today easily make excuses for doing.

TEACHER NOTES / CORRECTIONS

DAY - 20

✳[/3]

08. Give two examples of transgressions that someone might commit towards other people and their rights.

_____

_____

_____

_____

_____

_____

_____

_____

_____

_____

_____

_____

_____

_____

_____

_____

_____

DAY - 20

_____

_____

_____

_____

TEACHER NOTES / CORRECTIONS

_____

_____

_____

_____

_____

09. How many of the mentioned conditions for repentance are only or exclusively related to inward matters?

TEACHER NOTES / CORRECTIONS

TEST YOUR UNDERSTANDING

TRUE & FALSE QUESTIONS

[Circle the correct letter for each individual sentence from today's content.]

01. Shaytaan specifically directs his efforts at those Muslims who [T / F]
    are striving and growing in emaan.

02. The Companions of the Prophet, were blessed to not have to [T / F]
    face whispers from Shaytaan.

03. The Prophet's guidance for all Muslims includes the remedy to [T / F]
    Shaytaan's whispers and other deceptions.

FILL IN THE BLANK QUESTIONS

[Enter the correct individual words to complete the sentences from today's content.]

04. The _____, that a Muslim encounters from _____,
    are an evidence of _____ within his emaan or faith.

05. After seeking _____ in Allaah from Shaytaan's whispers a
    Muslim should not _____ any _____ to them and
    _____ they will subside and fade away.

06. A striving Muslim should expect _____, as long as what is in
    your heart remains _____ upon Islaam.

COMPREHENSIVE UNDERSTANDING QUESTIONS

7-12 min

07.   What is a common false idea or claim about Islaam that Shaytaan spreads among the people today?

_____

_____

_____

_____

_____

_____

_____

_____

_____

_____

_____

_____

_____

_____

_____

_____

_____

_____

_____

_____

_____

DAY - 21

TEACHER NOTES / CORRECTIONS

*[/3]

08. What are the two steps mentioned to ensure that the whispers of Shaytaan do not truly harm you at all?

_____

_____

_____

_____

_____

_____

_____

_____

_____

_____

_____

_____

_____

_____

_____

_____

_____

_____

_____

DAY - 21

_____

_____

_____

TEACHER NOTES / CORRECTIONS

_____

_____

_____

_____

_____

09. Give a practical example of how beneficial knowledge helps protect us against the deceptions of Shaytaan?

TEACHER NOTES / CORRECTIONS

*[/ 3]=[/ 15]

TEST YOUR UNDERSTANDING

TRUE & FALSE QUESTIONS

[Circle the correct letter for each individual sentence from today's content.]

3min

01. Whispers from Shaytaan of things that are against true sound belief do not throw you into disbelief. [T / F]

02. There are two clear steps to take when Shaytaan directs misguiding whispers towards your heart. [T / F]

03. Shaytaan only attacks those Muslims whose emaan, inwardly and outwardly, is already weak, as they are easy to harm. [T / F]

FILL IN THE BLANK QUESTIONS

[Enter the correct individual words to complete the sentences from today's content.]

6min

DAY - 22

04. _____ the _____ doubts from Shaytaan, is something extremely _____ for a Muslim.

05. Shaytaan uses _____ towards Muslims in order to _____ doubts and _____ their faith.

06. After seeking _____ in _____, a Muslim should not pay _____ or _____ upon whispered doubts.

COMPREHENSIVE UNDERSTANDING QUESTIONS

7-12 min

07.   Give an example of another source of doubts about correct belief, other than whispers, that a Muslim might encounter. How can a Muslim protect himself from that source you mentioned?

_____

_____

_____

_____

_____

_____

_____

_____

_____

_____

_____

_____

_____

_____

_____

_____

_____

_____

_____

DAY - 22

_____

_____

_____

TEACHER NOTES / CORRECTIONS

_____

_____

_____

_____

08. Give a specific example of possible way to not focus upon whispered doubts, after seeking refuge in Allaah.

TEACHER NOTES / CORRECTIONS

09. What evidence from the source texts in the lesson, gives us insight into one strategy of Shaytaan to lead a Muslim towards disbelief? Describe that strategy briefly.

DAY - 22

TEACHER NOTES / CORRECTIONS

*[/ 3] = [/ 15]

TEST YOUR UNDERSTANDING

TRUE & FALSE QUESTIONS

[Circle the correct letter for each individual sentence from today's content.]

3 min

01.   Only the Muslims of later times, due to our weakness, face   [T / F]
      whispers from Shaytaan.

02.   If we follow the guidance of the Sunnah, then the whispers we   [T / F]
      deal with properly, will go away and not actually harm us.

03.   A Muslim facing whispered doubts should sit and recite specific   [T / F]
      verses of the Qur'aan to fight against this.

FILL IN THE BLANK QUESTIONS

[Enter the correct individual words to complete the sentences from today's content.]

6 min

04.   Good endeavors, may be related to _____ _____
      efforts or seeking the _____ of the _____.

05.   Shaytaan wants to ruin a Muslim's inward _____ and his
      strong _____ to the _____.

06.   A striving Muslim must _____ and _____ the
      whispers from _____.

DAY - 23

COMPREHENSIVE UNDERSTANDING QUESTIONS

7-12 min

07.   Why are the presence of whispers of doubts not considered a sign of hypocrisy or of weak emaan?

DAY - 23

TEACHER NOTES / CORRECTIONS

*[/ 3]

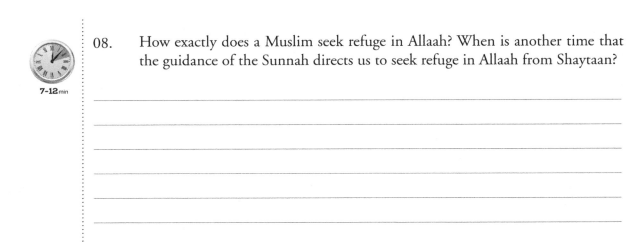

08. How exactly does a Muslim seek refuge in Allaah? When is another time that the guidance of the Sunnah directs us to seek refuge in Allaah from Shaytaan?

7-12 min

TEACHER NOTES / CORRECTIONS

09. Why was Ibn 'Abbaas not surprised that a disbeliever mentioned that he does not have to deal with whispers of Shaytaan?

TEACHER NOTES / CORRECTIONS

*[/ 3]=[/ 15]

TEST YOUR UNDERSTANDING

TRUE & FALSE QUESTIONS

[Circle the correct letter for each individual sentence from today's content.]

3 min

01. There are only some sins that you can repent from; other major [T / F] sins cause you to remain in Hellfire.

02. As long as a Muslim stops committing a sin, they do not have [T / F] to feel bad about having committing that wrongdoing.

03. If a person repents at the final point when already dying, their [T / F] repentance can still benefit them.

FILL IN THE BLANK QUESTIONS

[Enter the correct individual words to complete the sentences from today's content.]

6 min

04. Repentance has _____ that must be _____ and realized when _____ to Allaah.

05. Repentance done _____ for the sake of Allaah alone, means seeking to be saved from His _____, and hoping that it brings you towards His _____.

06. If someone plans to _____ to committing his sin after some _____, or in a certain _____, this _____ the fourth condition of repentance.

DAY - 24

COMPREHENSIVE UNDERSTANDING QUESTIONS

7-12min

07.　Is the first condition of repentance inward or outward? Give a specific example of how some might negate the first condition of repentance for a sin or transgression.

DAY - 24

TEACHER NOTES / CORRECTIONS

✳[　/3]

08. Give a specific example, other than those mentioned, of how someone might not fulfill or negate the third condition of repentance for a sin or transgression.

_____

_____

_____

_____

_____

_____

_____

_____

_____

_____

_____

_____

_____

_____

_____

_____

_____

_____

_____

_____

_____

_____

DAY - 24

TEACHER NOTES / CORRECTIONS

_____

_____

_____

_____

_____

_____

[/ 3]✱

09. Is the fourth condition of repentance inward or outward? Give a specific example of how someone might not fulfill the forth condition of repentance for a sin or transgression.

TEACHER NOTES / CORRECTIONS

107

*[/ 3]=[/ 15]

TEST YOUR UNDERSTANDING

TRUE & FALSE QUESTIONS

[Circle the correct letter for each individual sentence from today's content.]

3 min

01. As Muslims, we can keep money we earned from prohibited [T / F] means as long as our intention is to use it for Islaam.

02. Once a Muslim repents from the sin of unlawful earning, what [T / F] should further be done depends on his circumstances.

03. After repenting when a Muslim, who earned unlawful wealth, [T / F] gives it away, he gets the reward of that as charity.

FILL IN THE BLANK QUESTIONS

[Enter the correct individual words to complete the sentences from today's content.]

6 min

04. Giving away _____ earned wealth _____ _____ fulfill a person's individual _____ such as zakaat.

05. By _____ away illegally earned wealth, a Muslim who has _____ seeks to _____ themselves from that prohibited wealth.

06. Wealth earned in a _____ way can be donated to build a _____, or given away in _____, or for some endeavor generally _____ to Allaah.

DAY - 25

[/6]*

COMPREHENSIVE UNDERSTANDING QUESTIONS

7-12 min

07. Give an example of a prohibited way of earning wealth that can be seen today. What is an example of a permissible alternative to that.

_____

_____

_____

_____

_____

_____

_____

_____

_____

_____

_____

_____

_____

_____

_____

_____

_____

_____

_____

_____

_____

_____

TEACHER NOTES / CORRECTIONS

DAY - 25

_____

_____

_____

_____

*[/ 3]

08. What are two examples of possible community projects, not yet mentioned, that a Muslim should support to strengthen Islaam and the Muslims?

_____

_____

_____

_____

_____

_____

_____

_____

_____

_____

_____

_____

_____

_____

_____

_____

_____

_____

_____

_____

_____

_____

_____

_____

TEACHER NOTES / CORRECTIONS

_____

_____

_____

_____

_____

09. Why do we say that the wealth earned in a prohibited way is not accepted as a good deed by Allaah, even when the person had a good intention in what they were doing?

TEACHER NOTES / CORRECTIONS

✳[/ 3]=[/ 15]

TEST YOUR UNDERSTANDING

TRUE & FALSE QUESTIONS

[Circle the correct letter for each individual sentence from today's content.]

01. The Muslim who is repenting from wrongly taking someone's [T / F] money, should now just give that amount in charity.

02. One that person whose money you wrongfully took dies, there [T / F] is nothing left that you can do.

03. If you wronged someone's honor and reputation by lying and [T / F] slandering them, you only need to repent to Allaah.

FILL IN THE BLANK QUESTIONS

[Enter the correct individual words to complete the sentences from today's content.]

04. Whenever a person commits _____ their emaan or faith _____, and they become _____ away from their Lord.

05. It is suitable that the _____ person chooses to _____ his Muslim _____ who came to him seeking his pardon.

06. When someone who wrongly took money cannot _____ it, and gives that amount in _____, the reward of that charity goes to the _____ person.

COMPREHENSIVE UNDERSTANDING QUESTIONS

7-12min

07. Give a specific example of how someone might wrongly take someone's wealth in a business.

_____

_____

_____

_____

_____

_____

_____

_____

_____

_____

_____

_____

_____

_____

_____

_____

_____

_____

_____

_____

_____

_____

_____

_____

TEACHER NOTES / CORRECTIONS

DAY - 26

✳[/3]

7-12 min

08. Give the possible example of how someone might harm someone else's honor and reputation.

_____

_____

_____

_____

_____

_____

_____

_____

_____

_____

_____

_____

_____

_____

_____

_____

_____

_____

_____

_____

_____

_____

_____

_____

_____

_____

TEACHER NOTES / CORRECTIONS

DAY - 26

_____

_____

_____

_____

_____

[/3]✶

09. What might be a possible benefit of publicly speaking well about someone to the same people, and in the same places, that you previously wrongly spoke badly about them?

_____

TEACHER NOTES / CORRECTIONS

✻[/3]=[/15]

TEST YOUR UNDERSTANDING

TRUE & FALSE QUESTIONS

[Circle the correct letter for each individual sentence from today's content.]

3min

01. Whether a person is successful in being steadfast is completely [T / F] in their own control, with no other factors.

02. If someone is steadfast as a Muslim then, those who he interacts [T / F] with cannot affect that steadfastness.

03. A Muslim, along with his struggling and striving to stay away [T / F] from everything prohibited, must ask for Allaah to help him in these efforts.

FILL IN THE BLANK QUESTIONS

[Enter the correct individual words to complete the sentences from today's content.]

6min

04. A Muslim should looking closely at the _____, which come from obeying Allaah, and remember the _____, which result from this in this _____ and the _____.

05. Looking _____ at the _____ consequences of _____ the commands of Allaah and His Messenger, will _____ someone to better turn away from what has been prohibited,

06. The Prophet, may the praise and salutations of Allaah be upon him, _____ against _____ _____ with people involved in _____ and wrongdoing.

COMPREHENSIVE UNDERSTANDING QUESTIONS

7-12 min

07.   Give an example of a specific sin, and then list at least one possible bad consequence coming from it in this world, and one bad consequence in the Hereafter.

_____

_____

_____

_____

_____

_____

_____

_____

_____

_____

_____

_____

_____

_____

_____

_____

_____

_____

_____

_____

_____

_____

_____

TEACHER NOTES / CORRECTIONS

DAY - 27

✳[/ 3]

7-12min

08. Give an example of a specific act of obedience, and then list at least one possible good consequence coming from it in this world, and one good consequence the Hereafter.

TEACHER NOTES / CORRECTIONS

09. Give a specific example of one possible small negative effect of sitting with a bad companion, and one possible major or serious effect of sitting with a bad companion.

TEACHER NOTES / CORRECTIONS

DAY - 27

*[/ 3]=[/ 15]

TEST YOUR UNDERSTANDING

TRUE & FALSE QUESTIONS

[Circle the correct letter for each individual sentence from today's content.]

3 min

01. There is not really a difference between wara'a and zuhd, as [T / F] they are both concerned with the same thing.

02. Zuhd, requires significant effort, care, and consideration [T / F] regarding your entire life.

03. The Muslim with zuhd or with wara'a both stay away from all [T / F] prohibited matters, that they have knowledge of, completely.

FILL IN THE BLANK QUESTIONS

[Enter the correct individual words to complete the sentences from today's content.]

6 min

04. The person with wara'a _____ engages in those _____ matters which are _____, but not anything prohibited.

05. The person who is _____ as having zuhd, will also _____ _____ from _____ matters that don't have a specific benefit or reward in the Hereafter.

06. The person of zuhd stays away from those _____ matters because they _____ that _____ that they do in this life brings them some benefit in the _____ life.

COMPREHENSIVE UNDERSTANDING QUESTIONS

7-12 min

07. Give a specific example of something someone with wara'a might do, that was neutral and not prohibited for Muslims.

_____
_____
_____
_____
_____
_____
_____
_____
_____
_____
_____
_____
_____
_____
_____
_____
_____
_____
_____
_____
_____
_____
_____
_____
_____

TEACHER NOTES / CORRECTIONS

DAY - 28

✳[/ 3]

7-12min

08. Give a specific example of something someone with zuhd might turn away from, because it brought him no reward or benefit in the Hereafter.

_____
_____
_____
_____
_____
_____
_____
_____
_____
_____
_____
_____
_____
_____
_____
_____
_____
_____
_____
_____
_____
_____
_____
_____

TEACHER NOTES / CORRECTIONS

_____
_____
_____
_____
_____

DAY - 28

[/3]✳

09.   Give examples of three small simple acts of obedience that a Muslim can do with their time that will benefit them on the Day of Resurrection.

_____

_____

_____

_____

_____

_____

_____

_____

_____

_____

_____

_____

_____

_____

_____

_____

_____

_____

_____

_____

_____

_____

_____

_____

TEACHER NOTES / CORRECTIONS

DAY - 28

*[/ 3]=[/ 15]

TEST YOUR UNDERSTANDING

TRUE & FALSE QUESTIONS

[Circle the correct letter for each individual sentence from today's content.]

3min

01. The Muslims who are very pious and righteous focus only on   [T / F]
    making dhikr, and generally are secluded in private worship.

02. The best worshippers of Allaah are those who turn away from   [T / F]
    seeking the permissible things of this world.

03. Worshipping Allaah can be done in any way that someone feels   [T / F]
    acceptable and wants to focus upon.

FILL IN THE BLANK QUESTIONS

[Enter the correct individual words to complete the sentences from today's content.]

6min

04. _____ people _____ understand who are the true
    _____ worshipers of Allaah.

05. _____ good comes from those Muslims _____ earning
    _____ wealth, and then spending it upon what is beneficial
    for the Muslims.

06. Some people _____ believe that a righteous Muslim should
    generally _____ themselves from everyone and not be
    concerned with _____ what is good, or _____
    wrongdoing and evil.

COMPREHENSIVE UNDERSTANDING QUESTIONS

7-12min

07.   Explain any common misunderstanding about what is or is not properly considered worship, and give a practical example.

TEACHER NOTES / CORRECTIONS

08.   Give three additional ways that a Muslim can use permissibly earned wealth to benefit Islaam and the Muslims.

_____

_____

_____

_____

_____

_____

_____

_____

_____

_____

_____

_____

_____

_____

_____

_____

_____

_____

_____

_____

_____

_____

_____

TEACHER NOTES / CORRECTIONS

09. What is a fundamental reason that any people who intentionally withdraw themselves from most people, and generally don't interact with others, are misguided. Give one proof from the Qur'aan or Sunnah to support your answer.

_____
_____
_____
_____
_____
_____
_____
_____
_____
_____
_____
_____
_____
_____
_____
_____
_____
_____
_____
_____
_____
_____

TEACHER NOTES / CORRECTIONS

_____
_____
_____
_____

DAY - 29

*[/ 3]=[/ 15]

TEST YOUR UNDERSTANDING

TRUE & FALSE QUESTIONS

[Circle the correct letter for each individual sentence from today's content.]

3 min

01. There is a difference between wrongdoing in Islaam and the   [T / F]
     results or consequences of that wrongdoing.

02. Since the Muslims have fallen into weakness and humiliation,   [T / F]
     there is nothing they can do to change that condition except
     supplicate for a change from Allaah.

03. The state of emaan or faith of many Muslims today, is in fact   [T / F]
     inwardly and outwardly weak.

FILL IN THE BLANK QUESTIONS

[Enter the correct individual words to complete the sentences from today's content.]

6 min

04. Practices and matters which _____ the guidance of the
     _____ cause a _____ in our emaan or faith.

05. Humiliation is what Allaah's has _____ and _____
     for those who commit _____ and are far from practicing
     _____ correctly.

06. It is possible for the Muslims to _____ to a position of
     honor and _____, if they truly _____ back to
     _____ Allaah's revealed religion _____.

COMPREHENSIVE UNDERSTANDING QUESTIONS

7-12 min

07. Give an example of a recent development that is the result of some Muslims increasing in harm due to their ignorance or opposition to the guidance of Islaam.

_____

_____

_____

_____

_____

_____

_____

_____

_____

_____

_____

_____

_____

_____

_____

_____

_____

_____

_____

_____

_____

_____

TEACHER NOTES / CORRECTIONS

_____

_____

_____

_____

DAY - 30

*[/ 3]

08. Give an example of a continuing situation of humiliation that the Muslims face that reflects their weakness in the present age.

TEACHER NOTES / CORRECTIONS

09. Why is it important that Muslims understand the mentioned difference between just being within Islaam and truly having strong emaan?

TEACHER NOTES / CORRECTIONS

*[/ 3]=[/ 15]

THE NAKHLAH EDUCATIONAL SERIES:

The Purpose of the 'Nakhlah Educational Series' is to contribute to the present knowledge based efforts which enable Muslim individuals, families, and communities to understand and learn Islaam and then to develop within and truly live Islaam. Our commitment and goal is to contribute beneficial publications and works that:

Firstly, reflect the priority, message and methodology of all the prophets and messengers sent to humanity, meaning that single revealed message which embodies the very purpose of life, and of human creation. As Allaah the Most High has said,

We sent a Messenger to every nation ordering them that they should worship Allaah alone, obey Him and make their worship purely for Him, and that they should avoid everything worshipped besides Allaah. So from them there were those whom Allaah guided to His religion, and there were those who were unbelievers for whom misguidance was ordained. So travel through the land and see the destruction that befell those who denied the Messengers and disbelieved.—(Surah an-Nahl: 36)

Sheikh Rabee'a ibn Haadee al-Madkhalee in his work entitled, '*The Methodology of the Prophets in Calling to Allaah, That is the Way of Wisdom and Intelligence.*' explains the essential, enduring message of all the prophets:

"*So what was the message which these noble, chosen men, may Allaah's praises and salutations of peace be upon them all, brought to their people? Indeed their mission encompassed every matter of good and distanced and restrained every matter of evil. They brought forth to mankind everything needed for their well-being and happiness in this world and the Hereafter. There is nothing good except that they guided the people towards it, and nothing evil except that they warned the people against it. ...*

This was the message found with all of the Messengers; that they should guide to every good and warn against every evil. However where did they start, what did they begin with and what did they concentrate upon? There are a number of essentials, basic principles, and fundamentals which all their calls were founded upon, and which were the starting point for calling the people to Allaah. These fundamental points and principles are: 1. The worship of Allaah alone without any associates 2. The sending of prophets to guide creation 3. The belief in the resurrection and the life of the Hereafter

These three principles are the area of commonality and unity within their calls, and stand as the fundamental principles which they were established upon. These principles are given the greatest importance in the Qur'aan and are fully explained in it. They are also its most important purpose upon which it centers and which it continually mentions. It further quotes intellectual and observable proofs for them in all its chapters as well as within most of its accounts of previous nations and given examples.

This is known to those who have full understanding, and are able to consider carefully and comprehend well. All the Books revealed by Allaah have given great importance to these points and all of the various revealed laws of guidance are agreed upon them. And the most important and sublime of these three principles, and the most fundamental of them all is directing one's worship only towards Allaah alone, the Blessed and the Most High."

Today one finds that there are indeed many paths, groups, and organizations apparently presenting themselves as representing Islaam, which struggle to put forth an outwardly pleasing appearance to the general Muslims; but when their methods are placed upon the precise scale of conforming to priorities and methodology of the message of the prophets sent by Allaah, they can only be recognized as deficient paths- not simply in practice but in principle- leading not to success but rather only to inevitable failure. As Sheikh Saaleh al-Fauzaan, may Allaah preserve him, states in his introduction to the same above mentioned work on the methodology of all the prophets,

"So whichever call is not built upon these foundations, and whatever methodology is not from the methodology of the Messengers - then it will be frustrated and fail, and it will be effort and toil without any benefit. The clearest proofs of this are those present day groups and organizations which set out a methodology and program for themselves and their efforts of calling the people to Islaam which is different from the methodology of the Messengers. These groups have neglected the importance of the people having the correct belief and creed - except for a very few of them - and instead call for the correction of side-issues."

There can be no true success in any form for us as individuals, families, or larger communities without making the encompassing worship of Allaah alone, with no partners or associates, the very and only foundation of our lives. It is necessary that each individual knowingly choose to base his life upon that same foundation taught by all the prophets and messengers sent by the Lord of all the worlds, rather than simply delving into the assorted secondary concerns and issues invited to by the various numerous parties, innovated movements, and groups. Indeed Sheikh al-Albaanee, may Allaah have mercy upon him, stated:

"...We unreservedly combat against this way of having various different parties and groups. As this false way- of group or organizational allegiances - conforms to the statement of Allaah the Most High, **But they have broken their religion among them into sects, each group rejoicing in what is with it as its beliefs. And every party is pleased with whatever they stand with.** *–(Surah al-Mu'minoon: 53) And in truth they are no separate groups and parties in Islaam itself. There is only one true party, as is stated in a verse in the Qur'an,* **Verily, it is the party of Allaah that will be the successful.** *–(Surah al-Mujadilaah: 58). The party of Allaah are those people who stand with the Messenger of Allaah, may Allaah's praise and salutations be upon him, meaning that an individual proceeds upon the methodology of the Companions of the Messenger. Due to this we call for having sound knowledge of the Book and the Sunnah."*

(Knowledge Based Issues & Sharee'ah Rulings: The Rulings of The Guiding Scholar Sheikh Muhammad Naasiruddeen al-Albaanee Made in the City of Medina & In the Emirates – [Emiratee Fatwa no 114. P.30])

Secondly, building upon the above foundation, our commitment is to contributing publications and works which reflect the inherited message and methodology of the acknowledged scholars of the many various branches of Sharee'ah knowledge who stood upon the straight path of preserved guidance in every century and time since the time of our Messenger, may Allaah's praise and salutations be upon him. These people of knowledge, who are the inheritors of the Final Messenger, have always adhered closely to the two revealed sources of guidance: the Book of Allaah and the Sunnah of the Messenger of Allaah- may Allaah's praise and salutations be upon him, upon the united consensus, standing with the body of guided Muslims in every century - preserving and transmitting the true religion generation after generation. Indeed the Messenger of Allaah, may Allaah's praise and salutations be upon him, informed us that, *{ A group of people amongst my Ummah will remain obedient to Allaah's orders. They will not be harmed by those who leave them nor by those who oppose them, until Allaah's command for the Last Day comes upon them while they remain on the right path. }* (Authentically narrated in Saheeh al-Bukhaaree).

We live in an age in which the question frequently asked is, "*How do we make Islaam a reality?*" and perhaps the related and more fundamental question is, "*What is Islaam?*", such that innumerable different voices quickly stand to offer countless different conflicting answers through books, lectures, and every available form of modern media. Yet the only true course of properly understanding this question and its answer- for ourselves and our families -is to return to the criterion given to us by our beloved Messenger, may Allaah's praise and salutations be upon him. Indeed the Messenger of Allaah, may Allaah's praise and salutations be upon him, indicated in an authentic narration, clarifying the matter beyond doubt, that the only "Islaam" which enables one to be truly successful and saved in this world and the next is as he said, *{...that which I am upon and my Companions are upon today.}* (authentically narrated in Jaam'ea at-Tirmidhee) referring to that Islaam which stands upon unchanging revealed knowledge. While every other changed and altered form of Islaam, whether through some form of extremism or negligence, or through the addition or removal of something, regardless of whether that came from a good intention or an evil one- is not the religion that Allaah informed us abou when He revealed, ◈ *This day, those who disbelieved have given up all hope of your religion; so fear them not, but fear Me. This day, I have perfected your religion for you, completed My Favor upon you, and have chosen for you Islaam as your religion.*◈–(Surah al-Maa'idah: 3)

The guiding scholar Sheikh al-Albaanee, may have mercy upon him, said,

"*...And specifically mentioning those among the callers who have taken upon themselves the guiding of the young Muslim generation upon Islaam, working to educate them with its education, and to socialize them with its culture. Yet they themselves have generally not attempted to unify their understanding of those matters about Islaam regarding which the people of Islaam today differ about so severely.*

MISSION

And the situation is certainly not as is falsely supposed by some individuals from among them who are heedless or negligent - that the differences that exist among them are only in secondary matters without entering into or affecting the fundamental issues or principles of the religion; and the examples to prove that this is not true are numerous and recognized by those who have studied the books of the many differing groups and sects, or by the one who has knowledge of the various differing concepts and beliefs held by the Muslims today."(Mukhtasir al-'Uloo Lil'Alee al-Ghafaar, page 55)

Similarly he, may Allaah have mercy upon him, explained:

"Indeed, Islaam is the only solution, and this statement is something which the various different Islamic groups, organizations, and movements could never disagree about. And this is something which is from the blessings of Allaah upon the Muslims. However there are significant differences between the different Islamic groups, organizations, and movements that are present today regarding that domain which working within will bring about our rectification. What is that area of work to endeavor within, striving to restore a way of life truly reflecting Islaam, renewing that system of living which comes from Islaam, and in order to establish the Islamic government? The groups and movements significantly differ upon this issue or point. Yet we hold that it is required to begin with the matters of tasfeeyah —clarification, and tarbeeyah -education and cultivation, with both of them being undertaken together.

As if we were to start with the issue of governing and politics, then it has been seen that those who occupy themselves with this focus firstly posses beliefs which are clearly corrupted and ruined, and secondly that their personal behavior, from the aspect of conforming to Islaam, is very far from conforming to the actual guidance of the Sharee'ah. While those who first concern themselves with working just to unite the people and gather the masses together under a broad banner of the general term "Islaam", then it is seen that within the minds of those speakers who raise such calls -in reality there is fact no actual clear understanding of what Islaam is. Moreover, the understanding they have of Islaam has no significant impact in starting to change and reform their own lives. Due to this reason you find that many such individuals from here and there, who hold this perspective, are unable to truly realize or reflect Islaam even in areas of their own personal lives in matters which it is in fact easily possible for them to implement. As he holds that no one - regardless of whether it is because of his arrogance or pridefulness - can enter into directing him in an area of his personal life!

Yet at the same time these same individuals are raising their voices saying, "Judgment is only for Allaah!" and "It is required that judgment of affairs be according to what Allaah revealed." And this is indeed a true statement. But the one who does not possess something certainly cannot give or offer it to others. The majority of Muslims today have not established the judgment of Allaah fully upon themselves, yet they still seek from others to establish the judgment of Allaah within their governments...

...And I understand that this issue or subject is not immune from there being those who oppose our methodology of tasfeeyah and tarbeeyah. As there is the one who would say, "But establishing this tasfeeyah and tarbeeyah is a matter which requires many long years!" So, I respond by saying, this is not an important consideration in this matter, what is important is that we carry out what we have been commanded to do within our religion and by our Mighty Lord. What is important is that we begin by properly understanding our religion first and foremost. After this is accomplished then it will not be important whether the road itself is long or short.

And indeed I direct this statement of mine towards those men who are callers to the religion among the Muslims, and towards the scholars and those who direct our affairs. I call for them to stand upon complete knowledge of true Islaam, and to fight against every form of negligence and heedlessness regarding the religion, and against differing and disputes, as Allaah has said, ◆...and do not dispute with one another for fear that you lose courage and your strength departs ◆–(Surah Al-Anfaal: 46).

(Quoted from the work, 'The Life of Sheikh al-Albaanee, His Influence in Present Day Fields of Sharee'ah Knowledge, & the Praise of the Scholars for Him.' volume 1 page 380-385)

The guiding scholar Sheikh Zayd al-Madkhalee, may Allaah protect him, stated in his writing, 'The Well Established Principles of the Way of the First Generations of Muslims: It's Enduring & Excellent Distinct Characteristics' that,

"From among these principles and characteristics is that the methodology of tasfeeyah -or clarification, and tarbeeyah -or education and cultivation- is clearly affirmed and established as a true way coming from the first three generations of Islaam, and is something well known to the people of true merit from among them, as is concluded by considering all the related evidence. What is intended by tasfeeyah, when referring to it generally, is clarifying that which is the truth from that which is falsehood, what is goodness from that which is harmful and corrupt, and when referring to its specific meanings it is distinguishing the noble Sunnah of the Prophet and the people of the Sunnah from those innovated matters brought into the religion and the people who are supporters of such innovations.

As for what is intended by tarbeeyah, it is calling all of the creation to take on the manners and embrace the excellent character invited to by that guidance revealed to them by their Lord through His worshiper and Messenger Muhammad, may Allaah's praise and salutations be upon him; so that they might have good character, manners, and behavior. As without this they cannot have a good life, nor can they put right their present condition or their final destination. And we seek refuge in Allaah from the evil of not being able to achieve that rectification."

Thus the methodology of the people of standing upon the Prophet's Sunnah, and proceeding upon the 'way of the believers' in every century is reflected in a focus and concern with these two essential matters: tasfeeyah or clarification of what is original, revealed message from the Lord of all the worlds, and tarbeeyah or education and raising of ourselves, our families, and our communities, and our lands upon what has been distinguished to be that true message and path.

The Roles of the Scholars & General Muslims In Raising the New Generation

The priority and focus of the 'Nakhlah Educational Series' is reflected within in the following statements of Sheikh al-Albaanee, may Allaah have mercy upon him:

"As for the other obligation, then I intend by this the education of the young generation upon Islaam purified from all of those impurities we have mentioned, giving them a correct Islamic education from their very earliest years, without any influence of a foreign, disbelieving education."

(Silsilat al-Hadeeth ad-Da'eefah, Introduction page 2.)

"...And since the Messenger of Allaah, may Allaah's praise and salutations be upon him, has indicated that the only cure to remove this state of humiliation that we find ourselves entrenched within, is truly returning back to the religion. Then it is clearly obligatory upon us - through the people of knowledge- to correctly and properly understand the religion in a way that conforms to the sources of the Book of Allaah and the Sunnah, and that we educate and raise a new virtuous, righteous generation upon this."

(Clarification and Cultivation and the Need of the Muslims for Them)

It is essential in discussing our perspective upon this obligation of raising the new generation of Muslims, that we highlight and bring attention to a required pillar of these efforts as indicated by Sheikh al-Albaanee, may Allaah have mercy upon him, and others- in the golden words, *"through the people of knowledge"*. Since something we commonly experience today is that many people have various incorrect understandings of the role that the scholars should have in the life of a Muslim, failing to understand the way in which they fulfill their position as the inheritors of the Messenger of Allaah, may Allaah's praise and salutations be upon him, and stand as those who preserve and enable us to practice the guidance of Islaam. Indeed, the noble Imaam Sheikh as-Sa'dee, may Allaah have mercy upon him, in his work, *"A Definitive and Clear Explanation of the Work 'A Triumph for the Saved Sect'"* pages 237-240, has explained this crucial issue with an extraordinary explanation full of remarkable benefits:

"Section: Explaining the Conditions for These Two Source Texts to Suffice You -or the Finding of Sufficiency in these Two Sources of Revelation.

Overall the conditions needed to achieve this and bring it about return to two matters:

Firstly, the presence of the requirements necessary for achieving this; meaning a complete devotion to the Book and the Sunnah, and the putting forth of efforts both in seeking to understand their intended meanings, as well as in striving to be guided by them. What is required secondly is the pushing away of everything which prevents achieving this finding of sufficiency in them.

This is through having a firm determination to distance yourself from everything which contradicts these two source texts in what comes from the historical schools of jurisprudence, assorted various statements, differing principles and their resulting conclusions which the majority of people proceed upon. These matters which contradict the two sources of revelation include many affairs which, when the worshiper of Allaah repels them from himself and stands against them, the realm of his knowledge, understanding, and deeds then expands greatly. Through a devotion to them and a complete dedication towards these two sources of revelation, proceeding upon every path which assists one's understanding them, and receiving enlightenment from the light of the scholars and being guided by the guidance that they possess- you will achieve that complete sufficiency in them. And surely, in the positions they take towards the leading people of knowledge and the scholars, the people are three types of individuals:

The first of them is the one who goes to extremes in his attachment to the scholars. He makes their statements something which are infallible as if their words held the same position as those of the statements of the Messenger of Allaah, may Allaah's praise and salutations be upon him, as well as giving those scholars' statements precedence and predominance over the Book of Allaah and the Sunnah. This is despite the fact that every leading scholar who has been accepted by this Ummah was one who promoted and encouraged the following of the Book and the Sunnah, commanding the people not to follow their own statements nor their school of thought in anything which stood in opposition to the Book of Allaah and the Sunnah.

The second type is the one who generally rejects and invalidates the statements of the scholars and forbids the referring to the statements of the leading scholars of guidance and those people of knowledge who stand as brilliant lamps in the darkness. This type of person neither relies upon the light of discernment with the scholars, nor utilizes their stores of knowledge. Or even if perhaps they do so, they do not direct thanks towards them for this. And this manner and way prohibits them from tremendous good. Furthermore, that which motivates such individuals to proceed in this way is their falsely supposing that the obligation to follow the Messenger of Allaah, may Allaah's praise and salutations be upon him, and the giving of precedence to his statements over the statements of anyone else, requires that they do without any reliance upon the statements of the Companions, or those who followed them in goodness, or those leading scholars of guidance within the Ummah. And this is a glaring and extraordinary mistake.

As indeed the Companions and the people of knowledge are the means and the agency between the Messenger of Allaah, may Allaah's praise and salutations be upon him, and his Ummah- in the transmission and spreading his Sunnah in regard to both its wording and texts as well as its meanings and understanding. Therefore the one who follows them in what they convey in this is guided through their understandings, receives knowledge from the light they possess, benefits from the conclusions they have derived from these sources -of beneficial meanings and explanations, as well as in relation to subtle matters which scarcely occur to the minds of some of the other people of knowledge, or barely comes to be discerned by their minds. Consequently, from the blessing of Allaah upon this Ummah is that He has given them these guiding scholars who cultivate and educate them upon two clear types of excellent cultivation.

The first category is education from the direction of ones knowledge and understanding. They educate the Ummah upon the more essential and fundamental matters before the more complex affairs. They convey the meanings of the Book and the Sunnah to the minds and intellects of the people through efforts of teaching which rectifies, and through composing various beneficial books of knowledge which a worshiper doesn't even have the ability to adequately describe what is encompassed within them of aspects of knowledge and benefits. Works which reflect the presence of a clear white hand in deriving guidance from the Book of Allaah and the Sunnah, and through the arrangement, detailed clarification, division and explanation, through the gathering together of explanations, comparisons, conditions, pillars, and explanations about that which prevents the fulfillment of matters, as well as distinguishing between differing meanings and categorizing various knowledge based benefits.

The second category is education from the direction of ones conduct and actions. They cultivate the peoples characters encouraging them towards every praiseworthy aspect of good character, through explaining its ruling and high status, and what benefits comes to be realized from it, clarifying the reasons and paths which enable one to attain it, as well as those affairs which prevent, delay or hinder someone becoming one distinguished and characterized by it. Because they, in reality, are those who bring nourishment to the hearts and the souls; they are the doctors who treat the diseases of the heart and its defects. As such they educate the people through their statements, actions as well as their general guided way. Therefore the scholars have a tremendous right over this Ummah. The portion of love and esteem, respect and honor, and thanks due to them because their merits and their various good efforts stand above every other right after establishing the right of Allaah, and the right of His Messenger, may Allaah's praise and salutations be upon him.

Because of this, the third group of individuals in respect to the scholars are those who have been guided to understand their true role and position, and establish their rights, thanking them for their virtues and merits, benefiting by taking from the knowledge they have, while acknowledging their rank and status. They understand that the scholars are not infallible and that their statements must stand in conformance to the statements of the Messenger of Allaah, may Allaah's praise and salutations be upon him. And that each one from among them has that which is from guidance, knowledge, and correctness in his statements taken and benefited from, while turning away from whatever in mistaken within it.

Yet such a scholar is not to be belittled for his mistake, as he stands as one who strove to reach the truth; therefore his mistake will be forgiven, and he should be thanked for his efforts. One clarifies what was stated by of any one of these leaders from among men, when it is recognizes that it has some weakness or conflict to an evidence of the Sharee'ah, by explaining its weakness and the level of that weakness, without speaking evilly of the intention of those people of knowledge and religion, nor defaming them due to that error. Rather we say, as it is obligatory to say, "And those who came after them say: ❦ **Our Lord! forgive us and our brethren who have preceded us in faith, and put not in our hearts any hatred against those who have believed. Our Lord! You are indeed full of kindness, Most Merciful.** ❦ -(Surah al-Hashr: 10).

Accordingly, individuals of this third type are those who fulfill two different matters. They join together on one hand between giving precedence to the Book and the Sunnah over everything else, and, on the other hand, between comprehending the level and position of the scholars and the leading people of knowledge and guidance, and establishing this even if it is only done in regard to some of their rights upon us. So we ask Allaah to bless us to be from this type, and to make us from among the people of this third type, and to make us from those who love Him and love those who love Him, and those who love every action which brings us closer to everything He loves."

Upon this clarity regarding the proper understanding of our balanced position towards our guided Muslim scholars, consider the following words about the realm of work of the general people of faith, which explains our area of efforts and struggle as Muslim parents, found in the following statement by Sheikh Saaleh Fauzaan al-Fauzaan, may Allaah preserve him.

"Question: Some people mistakenly believe that calling to Allaah is a matter not to be undertaken by anyone else other than the scholars without exception, and that it is not something required for other than the scholars according to that which they have knowledge of -to undertake any efforts of calling the people to Allaah. So what is your esteemed guidance regarding this?" The Sheikh responded by saying:

"This is not a misconception, but is in fact a reality. The call to Allaah cannot be established except through those who are scholars. And I state this. Yet, certainly there are clear issues which every person understands. As such, every individual should enjoin the good and forbid wrongdoing according to the level of his understanding. Such that he instructs and orders the members of his household to perform the ritual daily prayers and other matters that are clear and well known.

*Undertaking this is something mandatory and required even upon the common people, such that they must command their children to perform their prayers in the masjid. The Messenger of Allaah, may Allaah praise and salutations be upon him, said, { **Command you children to pray at seven, and beat them due to its negligence at ten.**} (Authentic narration found in Sunan Abu Dawood). And the Messenger of Allaah, may Allaah praise and salutations be upon him, said, { **Each one of you is a guardian or a shepherd, and each of you is responsible for those under his guardianship....**} (Authentic narration found in Saheeh al-Bukhaaree). So this is called guardianship, and this is also called enjoining the good and forbidding wrongdoing. The Messenger of Allaah, may Allaah praise and salutations be upon him, said, { **The one from among you who sees a wrong should change it with his hand, and if he is unable to do so, then with his tongue, and if he is not able to do this, then with his heart.** } (Authentic narration found in Saheeh Muslim).*

So in relation to the common person, that which it is required from him to endeavor upon is that he commands the members of his household-as well as others -with the proper performance of the ritual prayers, the obligatory charity, with generally striving to obey Allaah, and to stay away from sins and transgressions, and that he purify and cleanse his home from disobedience, and that he educate and cultivate his children upon the obedience of Allaah's commands. This is what is required from him, even if he is a general person. As these types of matters are from that which is understood by every single person. This is something which is clear and apparent.

MISSION

But as for the matters of putting forth rulings and judgments regarding matters in the religion, or entering into clarifying issues of what is permissible and what is forbidden, or explaining what is considered associating others in the worship due to Allaah and what is properly worshiping Him alone without any partner- then indeed these are matters which cannot be established except by the scholars"

(Beneficial Responses to Questions About Modern Methodologies, Question 15, page 22)

Similarly the guiding scholar Sheikh 'Abdul-'Azeez Ibn Baaz, may Allaah have mercy upon him, also emphasized this same overall responsibility:

"...It is also upon a Muslim that he struggles diligently in that which will place his worldly affairs in a good state, just as he must also strive in the correcting of his religious affairs and the affairs of his own family. As the people of his household have a significant right over him that he strive diligently in rectifying their affair and guiding them towards goodness, due to the statement of Allaah, the Most Exalted, **Oh you who believe! Save yourselves and your families Hellfire whose fuel is men and stones** *-(Surah at-Tahreem: 6)*

So it is upon you to strive to correct the affairs of the members of your family. This includes your wife, your children- both male and female- and such as your own brothers. This concerns all of the people in your family, meaning you should strive to teach them the religion, guiding and directing them, and warning them from those matters Allaah has prohibited for us. Because you are the one who is responsible for them as shown in the statement of the Prophet, may Allaah's praise and salutations be upon him, **{ Every one of you is a guardian, and responsible for what is in his custody. The ruler is a guardian of his subjects and responsible for them; a husband is a guardian of his family and is responsible for it; a lady is a guardian of her husband's house and is responsible for it, and a servant is a guardian of his master's property and is responsible for it....}** *Then the Messenger of Allaah, may Allaah's praise and salutations be upon him, continued to say,* **{...so all of you are guardians and are responsible for those under your authority.}** *(Authentically narrated in Saheeh al-Bukhaaree & Muslim)*

It is upon us to strive diligently in correcting the affairs of the members of our families, from the aspect of purifying their sincerity of intention for Allaah's sake alone in all of their deeds, and ensuring that they truthfully believe in and follow the Messenger of Allaah, may Allaah's praise and salutations be upon him, their fulfilling the prayer and the other obligations which Allaah the Most Exalted has commanded for us, as well as from the direction of distancing them from everything which Allaah has prohibited.

It is upon every single man and women to give advice to their families about the fulfillment of what is obligatory upon them. Certainly, it is upon the woman as well as upon the man to perform this. In this way our homes become corrected and rectified in regard to the most important and essential matters. Allaah said to His Prophet, may Allaah's praise and salutations be upon him, **And enjoin the ritual prayers on your family...** *(Surah Taha: 132) Similarly, Allaah the Most Exalted said to His prophet Ismaa'aeel,* **And mention in the Book, Ismaa'aeel. Verily, he was true to what he promised, and he was a Messenger, and a Prophet. And he used to enjoin on his family and his people the ritual prayers and the obligatory charity, and his Lord was pleased with him.** *-(Surah Maryam: 54-55)*

As such, it is only proper that we model ourselves after the prophets and the best of people, and be concerned with the state of the members of our households. Do not be neglectful of them, oh worshipper of Allaah! Regardless of whether it is concerning your wife, your mother, father, grandfather, grandmother, your brothers, or your children; it is upon you to strive diligently in correcting their state and condition..."

(Collection of Various Rulings and Statements- Sheikh 'Abdul-'Azeez Ibn 'Abdullah Ibn Baaz, Vol. 6, page 47)

MISSION

We hope to contribute works which enable every striving Muslim who acknowledges the proper position of the scholars, to fulfill the recognized duty and obligation which lays upon each one of us to bring the light of Islaam into our own lives as individuals as well as into our homes and among our families. Towards this goal we are committed to developing educational publications and comprehensive educational curricula -through cooperation with and based upon the works of the scholars of Islaam and the students of knowledge. Works which, with the assistance of Allaah, the Most High, we can utilize to educate and instruct ourselves, our families and our communities upon Islaam in both principle and practice. The publications and works of the Nakhlah Educational Series are divided into the following categories:

Basic / Elementary: Ages 4-11

Secondary: Ages 11-14

High School: Ages 14- Young Adult

General: Young Adult –Adult

Supplementary: All Ages

Publications and works within these stated levels will, with the permission of Allaah, encompass different beneficial areas and subjects, and will be offered in every permissible form of media and medium. As certainly, as the guiding scholar Sheikh Saaleh Fauzaan al-Fauzaan, may Allaah preserve him, has stated,

"Beneficial knowledge is itself divided into two categories. Firstly is that knowledge which is tremendous in its benefit, as it benefits in this world and continues to benefit in the Hereafter. This is religious Sharee'ah knowledge. And secondly, that which is limited and restricted to matters related to the life of this world, such as learning the processes of manufacturing various goods. This is a category of knowledge related specifically to worldly affairs.

…As for the learning of worldly knowledge, such as knowledge of manufacturing, then it is legislated upon us collectively to learn whatever the Muslims have a need for. Yet, if they do not have a need for this knowledge, then learning it is a neutral matter upon the condition that it does not compete with or displace any areas of Sharee'ah knowledge…"

("Explanations of the Mistakes of Some Writers"', Pages 10-12)

So we strive always to remind ourselves and our brothers of this crucial point also indicated by Sheikh Sadeeq Ibn Hasan al-Qanoojee, may Allaah have mercy upon him, in: *'Abjad al-'Uloom'*, (page 89)

"...What is intended by knowledge in the mentioned hadeeth is knowledge of the religion and the distinctive Sharee'ah, knowledge of the Noble Book and the pure Sunnah, of which there is no third along with them. But what is not meant in this narration are those invented areas of knowledge, whether they emerged in previous ages or today's world, which the people in these present times have devoted themselves to. They have specifically dedicated themselves to them in a manner which prevents them from looking towards those areas of knowledge related to faith, and in a way which has preoccupied them from occupying themselves from what is actually wanted or desired by Allaah, the Most High, and His Messenger, who is the leader of men and Jinn. Such that the knowledge in the Qur'aan has become something abandoned and the sciences of hadeeth have become obscure. While these new areas of knowledge related to manufacturing and production continually emerge from the nations of disbelief and apostasy, and they are called, "sciences", "arts", and "ideal development". And this sad state increases every day, indeed from Allaah we came and to Him shall we return....

...Additionally, although the various areas of beneficial knowledge all share some level of value, they all have differing importance and ranks. Among them is that which is to be considered according to its subject, such as medicine, and its subject is the human body. Or such as the sciences of 'tafseer' and its subject is the explanation of the words of Allaah, the Most Exalted and Most High, and the value of these two areas is not in any way unrecognized.

And from among the various areas there are those areas which are considered according to their objective, such as knowledge of upright character, and its goal is understanding the beneficial merits that an individual can come to possess. And from among them there are those areas which are considered according to the people's need for them, such as 'fiqh' which the need for it is urgent and essential. And from among them there are those areas which are considered according to their apparent strength, such as knowledge of physical sports and exercise, as it is something openly demonstrated.

And from the areas of knowledge are those areas which rise in their position of importance through their combining all these different matters within them, or the majority of them. Such as revealed religious knowledge, as its subject is indeed esteemed, its objective one of true merit, and its need is undeniably felt. Likewise one area of knowledge may be considered of superior rank than another in consideration of the results that it brings forth, or the strength of its outward manifestation, or due to the essentialness of its objective. Similarly the result that an area produces is certainly of higher estimation and significance in appraisal than the outward or apparent significance of some other areas of knowledge.

For that reason the highest ranking and most valuable area of knowledge is that of knowledge of Allaah the Most Perfect and the Most High, of His angels, and messengers, and all the particulars of these beliefs, as its result is that of eternal and continuing happiness."

MISSION

We ask Allaah, the most High to bless us with success in contributing to the many efforts of our Muslim brothers and sisters committed to raising themselves as individuals and the next generation of our children upon that Islaam which Allaah has perfected and chosen for us, and which He has enabled the guided Muslims to proceed upon in each and every century. We ask him to forgive us, and forgive the Muslim men and the Muslim women, and to guide all the believers to everything He loves and is pleased with. The success is from Allaah, The Most High The Most Exalted, alone and all praise is due to Him.

Abu Sukhailah Khalil Ibn-Abelahyi
Taalib al-Ilm Educational Resources

Taalib al-Ilm Educational Publications is looking for

Distributors:

We are working to make Taalib al-Ilm Education Resources publications available through distributors worldwide. Our present discounts for wholesalers are:

50% discount for any order of **USD**   **$1000** or over retail cost

60% discount for any order of **USD**   **$2000** or over retail cost

For further information, please contact the sales department by e-mail: *service@taalib.com.*

Publication Contributors:

Additionally, in an effort to further expand our publication library, we are seeking contributing authors, translators, and compilers with beneficial works of any area of Sharee'ah knowledge for submission of their works for potential publication by us. For details and all submission guidelines please email us at: *service@taalib.com*

Referral bonus: *Individuals who refer a new distributor or publication contributor to us can receive a **$25 PayPal payment** upon:*

1) a confirmed contract with a publication contributor or

2) receipt of a newly referred distributor's initial order at the 50% discount level.

Contact us for further information and conditions.

MISSION

30 Days of Guidance [Book 2]:
Cultivating The Character & Behavior of Islaam

A Short Journey Within The Work Al-Adab Al-Mufrad With

Sheikh Zayd Ibn Muhammad Ibn Haadee al-Madhkhaalee
(may Allaah have mercy on him)

*Do you understand the nature of Islaam? * What do you have that is equal to this world? * Are you wealthy? * Are you prepared for your reckoning? * Are you always working for good while you can? * Do you remember the benefit in your difficulties? * Which of these two pairs has a greater influence in your life? * Whom do you really love and why? * Who are your close friends? * Do you protect yourself from the harm of others? * Are you a miser or someone who is incapable? * Do you know the best of supplications? * Do you ask Allaah's protection from your own evil? * Do you seek refuge from bad conditions and worship at night? * Do you know which trials contain some betterment for you? * Do you supplicate for your family as both a parent and as a child? * How well do you treat your mother and father? * How do you fulfill your responsibilities towards your household? * Do you know who are the best and worst of Muslim women? * Is your life balanced as was the lives of the Companions? * Do you understand how to give the best of charity? * How do you spend your money? * How many ways of giving charity and doing good do you do * How are you towards your neighbors? * How do you deal with your own faults and those of others? * How do you treat younger Muslims? * How do you interact with other Muslims? * Do you work to change your bad habits? * Do you know the benefits of maintaining family ties? * Do you know what things bring you closer to Jannah?*

Compiled and Translated by:

Abu Sukhailah Khalil Ibn-Abelahyi

[Available: **Now** ¦ price: **(SS) $27.50 (DS) $25 (W) $12** ¦ **(Kindle) $9.99**]

PREVIEW

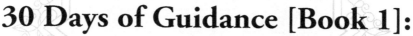

BELIEFS & WORSHIP

30 Days of Guidance [Book 1]:
Learning Fundamental Principles of Islaam

A Short Journey Within the Work al-Ibanah al-Sughrah With

Sheikh 'Abdul-Azeez Ibn 'Abdullah ar-Raajhee

(may Allaah preserve him)

*The Importance Of Asking To Be Guided In What You Say & Do * The Clear Guidance Of The Final Messenger Is For All Humanity * There Is A Single Straight Path Surrounded By Other False Paths * Every Ummah Divided But Those Upon The Truth Remain * Allaah Is With Those Who Remained Upon Revealed Guidance * Allaah Has Ordered Us To Stand United Upon The Truth & Not Divide * Every Name That Opposes The Guidance Of The Sunnah Is Rejected * The Strangeness Of Islaam Is Something Expected * That One Individual Whose Religion You Should Stand Upon * The Sunnah Is Revealed Knowledge From Allaah * Hold Firmly To The Sunnah As The Rope Of Allaah * Success Is To The Degree You Adhere To The Sunnah * The Incredible Reward For Firmly Holding To The Sunnah * Follow The Prophet's Sunnah & That Of His Guided Successors * Do Not Speak Against The Best Of Generations * Know That Knowledge Is Received And Can Be Lost * The Reality of the People of Misguidance & Their Deceptions * The Believers Are Distinct Upon Revealed Guidance * Advice of The Companions 'Uthman, 'Alee & Ibn 'Abbaas * Those Astray Turned Away From The Guidance Brought To Them * The People Of Misguidance Want You To Turn From Revealed Guidance * Those Who Debate Frequently Change Their Religion * The Blessing of Learning the Sunnah When Young * The Importance Of Both Loving & Hating For Allaah's Sake * A Person Stands Upon The Religion Of His Close Companion * Innovation That Is Disbelief Destroys All Ones' Good Deeds * Innovations In Islaam May Mislead You To Leave Islaam * The One Who Changes Islaam Is Cursed By Allaah & Creation * Repentance from Innovation Must Be Clear & Apparent * What Religion Will You Die Upon?*

Compiled and Translated by:
Abu Sukhailah Khalil Ibn-Abelahyi

[Available: **Now** ¦ price: **(SS) $27.50 (DS) $25 (W) $12** ¦ **(Kindle) $9.99**]

PREVIEW

An Educational Course Based Upon:

Beneficial Answers to Questions On Innovated Methodologies

By the Guiding Scholar

Sheikh Saaleh Ibn Abdullah al-Fauzaan

(may Allaah preserve him)

This course focuses upon the importance of clarity in the way you understand and practice Islaam, in the midst of today's confusing claims to Islaam.

What is the right way or methodology, to practice Islaam? Examine evidences and proofs from the sources texts of the Qur'aan and Sunnah along with the statements of many scholars explaining them, which connect you directly to that Islaam which the Messenger of Allaah ﷺ taught his Companions, may Allaah be pleased with them all.

Course Features:

Twenty concise illustrated lessons to facilitate learning & review with several important textual & course appendices.

Compiled and Translated by:

Abu Sukhailah Khalil Ibn-Abelahyi

[Available: **Now** ¦ price: **(SS) $35 (DS) $32.50 (W) $12** ¦ **(Kindle) $9.99**]

BELIEFS & WORSHIP

Lessons & Benefits From the Two Excellent Works:

The Belief of Every Muslim & The Methodology of The Saved Sect

By the Guiding Scholar

Sheikh Muhammad Ibn Jameel Zaynoo

(may Allaah preserve him)

This course begins with three full lessons with specific practical guidelines on how to effectively study Islaam and gain the knowledge needed to build your life as a Muslim into a life which is pleasing to Allaah.

Through twenty lessons on knowledge, beliefs, & methodology along with quizzes, review questions & lesson benefits -the remaining lessons take simply explained passages from two beneficial works that cover many important principles and the common misconceptions connected to them, which are fundamental to correctly understanding Islaam as it was taught to the Companions of the Messenger of Allaah.

Compiled and Translated by:

Abu Sukhailah Khalil Ibn-Abelahyi

[Available: **Now** ¦ price: (SS) **$27.50** (DS) **$25** (W) **$12** ¦ (Kindle) **$9.99**]

PREVIEW

Statements of the Guiding Scholars of Our Age

Regarding Books & their Advice to the Beginner Seeker of Knowledge

with Selections from the Following Scholars:

Sheikh 'Abdul-'Azeez ibn 'Abdullah ibn Baaz -Sheikh Muhammad ibn Saaleh al-'Utheimein - Sheikh Muhammad Naasiruddeen al-Albaanee - Sheikh Muqbil ibn Haadee al-Waada'ee - Sheikh 'Abdur-Rahman ibn Naaser as-Sa'adee - Sheikh Muhammad 'Amaan al-Jaamee - Sheikh Muhammad al-Ameen as-Shanqeetee - Sheikh Ahmad ibn Yahya an-Najmee

(May Allaah have mercy upon them)

Sheikh Saaleh al-Fauzaan ibn 'Abdullah al-Fauzaan - Sheikh Saaleh ibn 'Abdul-'Azeez Aal-Sheikh - Sheikh Muhammad ibn 'Abdul-Wahhab al-Wasaabee -Permanent Committee to Scholastic Research & Issuing Of Islamic Rulings
(May Allaah preserve them.)

Book Sections:

1. Guidance and Direction for Every Male and Female Muslim

2. Golden Advice that Benefits the Beginner Regarding Acquiring Knowledge

3. Beneficial Guidance for Female Students of Sharee'ah Knowledge

4 Guidance from the Scholars Regarding Important Books to Acquire for Seeking Knowledge

5. The Warning of the Scholars from the Books of those who have Deviated &
the Means and Ways of Going Astray

6. Clear Statements from the Scholars' Advice Regarding Memorizing Knowledge

7. Issues Related to the Verifiers of Books in our Age

Compiled and Translated by:

Abu Sukhailah Khalil Ibn-Abelahyi

[Available: **Now** ┊ price: **(HB) $32.50 (SB) $25**
┊ **(Kindle) $9.99**]

The Cure, The Explanation, The Clear Affair, & The Brilliantly Distinct Signpost [1]

A Step by Step Educational Course on Islaam
Based upon Commentaries of

'Usul as-Sunnah' of Imaam Ahmad

(may Allaah have mercy upon him)

This initial course book, which is part of a full series, can be vital learning tool, by Allah's persmission, for discussing and learning many of the most important beliefs of Islaam, how to implement them, and how to avoid common mistakes and misunderstandings. This full course series is based upon various commentaries of the original text, from the following scholars of our age, may Allaah preserve them all:

- Sheikh Zayd Ibn Muhammad al-Madkhalee
- Sheikh Saleeh Ibn Sa'd As-Suhaaymee
- Sheikh 'Abdul-'Azeez Ibn 'Abdullah ar-Raajhee
- Sheikh Rabee'a Ibn Haadee al-Madkhalee
- Sheikh Sa'd Ibn Naasir as-Shathree
- Sheikh 'Ubayd Ibn 'Abdullah al-Jaabiree
- Sheikh 'Abdullah Al-Bukharee
- Sheikh Hamaad Uthmaan

Each course book lesson has: lesson text, scholastic commentary, evidence summary, lesson benefits, standard & review exercises, as well as the Arabic text & translation of 'Usul as-Sunnah' in Arabic divided for easier memorization.

Compiled and Translated by:

Abu Sukhailah Khalil Ibn-Abelahyi

[Available: **TBA** ¦ price: **(SS) $30 (DS) $27.50 (W) $12** ¦ **(Kindle) $9.99**]

PREVIEW

30 Days of Guidance:
SIGNPOSTS TOWARDS RECTIFICATION & REPENTANCE

Book Description:

This is book 3 in our 30 Days Series. It is intended to assist any Muslim who wished to improve his life and that of those arround him through the perfect guidance of Islam.
It is divided into **30 daily** selections of one or more beneficial questions and answers from the estemed Sheikh Muhammad Ibn Saleh al-'Utheimeen, may Allah have mercy upon him, along with brief points of benefit and practical discussions on implementing his guidance related to repentance and self rectificationin our lives as Muslims commited to living Islaam. The importance of this subject has been indicated by many scholars of the Sunah past and present.The noble scholar Ibn al-Qayyim, may Allaah have mercy upon him, mentioned in his work 'Madaarij as-Saalikeen',

"The purification of the self or soul and its becoming rectified is dependent upon it being called to account and assessed. There is no purification or rectification nor any possibility of it being brought to a state of well-being except through calling oneself to account.
al-Hasan al-Basree, may Allaah have mercy upon him, said, "As for the believer, then you do not see him, in other state except as one who steps forth and confronts himself says:
Why did I make such and such statement? Why did I eat such and such food?
Why did I go to such and such place? What do I do this thing?
What did I engage in that matter? By Allaah, I will not fall into that again, and what is similar to theses statements. He takes himself to account looking at his shortcomings and deficiencies. So that he has the opportunity to try and fix, and rectify them

Yet this self rectification or purification of the soul must be done in the corect way and upon the correct foundation if it is to be successful. Ibn al-Qayyim, may Allaah have mercy upon him, also state "The true purification of the soul and the self is directly connected to those messengers sent to humanity. Certainly Allaah sent messengers for the purpose of this purification of souls, and commanded them to pursue this, and brought it about through their hands, through efforts of calling, teaching, and guiding the people. They were sent to guide the various nations of the earth..

...There is no path to truly cure and rectify the hearts except by means of their revealed paths and through their hands as messengers, and through purely surrendering and complying to their guidanc And we seek Allaah's assistance in our affairs"

TAALIB AL-ILM
EDUCATIONAL RESOURCES
LEARN ISLAAM, LIVE ISLAAM
http://taalib.com

INCLUDES COURSE CERTIFICATE

30 Days OF GUIDANCE Series BOOK THREE

ISBN 9781938117596
9 781938 117596
LPN RT D   0177